Bobby Sands
and the
Tragedy of Northern Ireland

JOHN M. FEEHAN

You have to be prepared to defend the things in which you believe and be prepared to use force to secure the future of liberty and self-determination.

MARGARET THATCHER MP

I0160236

THE MERCIER PRESS
DUBLIN and CORK

Mercier Press
www.mercierpress.ie

First published 1983

© the estate of John M. Feehan

ISBN 798 1 78117 854 6

Transferred to digital print on demand in 2023.

Dedicated to

Marcella and Bernadette

A CIP record for this title is available from the British Library.

Contents

A Word to the Reader

The idea of writing this book came to me at a variety of different times and in a variety of different ways. While I was researching my last book *The Shooting of Michael Collins,* I was intrigued by a number of strange and curious factors. I found that, by and large, newspaper accounts of particular events bore little relation to what actually happened. For example, according to the papers of the time there were two hundred ambushers at Béalnabláth and approximately fifty of them were casualties. The truth of course is that there were only five ambushers and none of them were casualties. The more I looked at other events of the period I found that this type of misinformation was widespread. Hardly any event was reported accurately. During the Anglo-Irish War things were reported so as to favour the British and during the Civil War the news was reported to favour the Free State regime. In both cases it was slanted in favour of the reigning government.

Northern Ireland was now very much to the fore and I wondered if it were possible that things had not changed and that the diet of news we were getting about Northern Ireland was also false?

There was something else too which I found quite remarkable. The present day IRA was being loudly condemned by almost everyone of standing in the community: bishops, priests, public officials, academics, politicians. I found it intriguing to read in the old newspapers that it was the same categories of people who condemned Pearse, De Valera, Collins and others during the Anglo-Irish War. More interesting still was the fact that the very words which these people are using today, 'thug, murderer, criminal', are the same words which were used half-a-century ago to describe individuals who a short time later were to be revered as men of the highest honour and integrity. So to my ordinary and commonplace mind there was something here that did not quite add up. If these men of the past were really criminals how could they all miraculously turn into saints a few months or a few years later? Or could there be some truth in Napoleon's remark that 'God is on the side of the victors'? Could it be that those now being condemned as criminals would, over the next few years, be respected by their present critics as men of uprightness and rectitude? Had this not happened before and could it not happen again? Could it really be that the standards by which the critics judged people and events were such that they could be trimmed to suit every wind? Or could it be that I myself was thinking in a very naïve way?

So I decided to take a closer look at my own attitude to the whole question of Northern Ireland. A long life has taught me that it is wiser to accept the advice of the Gospels and search for the beam in one's own eye before casting around for the mote in somebody else's. The first question then that presented itself to me was: *What did I, as an average Southern Irishman, believe about the North?*

This was not difficult to answer. I believed that there were injustices in Northern Ireland and that both the British and Unionists were responsible for these injustices. But everything was so very far away it never occurred to me that the Southern government could be in any way guilty. I believed that the IRA were fighting for a Thirty-two County Republic in a misguided way and I also believed that they had no mandate from the people of Ireland to engage in such a fight. As well as that I believed they had committed some very unnecessary killings. Again it did not occur to me that Pearse, Connolly, Clarke, De Valera and Collins had no mandate either for the 1916 Rising or for the subsequent Anglo-Irish War and when it came to killing they had shown little mercy towards their opponents. But perhaps I was somewhat conditioned against the IRA? After all, as a young officer serving in the Irish Army during the Second World War I gave armed protection to the police when they were raiding IRA homes. I knew what it was to put the butt of a rifle into a door and tear a young man from his bed in the early hours of the morning in the presence of a distraught mother and perhaps subconsciously I had a certain understanding for those who were doing this in the North. Again without too close an examination, I believed in the Northern Ireland policy of Fianna Fáil and in the Republicanism of Jack Lynch and Charlie Haughey. Were they not carrying on the torch of freedom lit by De Valera when he founded Fianna Fáil in 1926? Their policy of a United Ireland with the consent of the Unionists and the British seemed a reasonable policy. Again it did not occur to me to ask when or under what circumstances such a consent would be given. Nor did it occur to me to ask myself what happens to the half-a-million Nationalists in the meantime? Neither did it occur to me to read the speech of Eamon de Valera at the La Scala Theatre in May 1926 when he founded Fianna Fáil and to compare that speech with the present day actions of his successors. Had I done so I would have had quite a surprise in store. Yet despite this woolly thinking on my part and despite the fact that these comforting beliefs of mine were fed and nurtured by the media there were recurring doubts hovering around the fringes of my mind.

Apart from the doubts caused by my own research on Collins, whispers of brutal torture, inhuman treatment, intimidation and other disturbing things began to trickle through and be talked about. These whispers were fanned by some outspoken editorials and features which very occasionally appeared in certain responsible newspapers, journals and programmes. Could it be that, like the reports of the Béalnabláth ambush, I, as well as the general public, had been taken for a ride?

I suppose the real moment of decision came for me when young Bobby Sands, an elected member of the British parliament, died in Long Kesh after sixty-six days on hunger-strike. I cannot say that I had much sympathy with Bobby Sands. After all, I felt, he did not have to die. Did not the Cardinal Archbishop of Westminster, Basil Hume say that, because Sands could have saved himself and did not, his act was an 'act of suicide'? I was inclined to accept the Cardinal's authoritative statement were it not for the fact that a disturbing and persistent thought kept bothering me: Jesus Christ could have saved his life when he came before Pilate, but he refused to do so. Did the founder of Christianity therefore commit suicide? Again, I had to face many more real and searching questions. Why did this young man starve to death? Why did more than thirty thousand decent citizens elect him as their MP? Do half-a-million people in all countries in the world march in public protest at the death of a criminal, as he was described by the British prime minister? Was it possible that Bobby Sands and the two thousand other men and women prisoners in Northern Ireland were all gangsters and pyschopaths?

There was only one way to answer these barbed doubts and that was to make as thorough an investigation as possible. And so to start with I asked myself the next question: *Where did I get my opinions and beliefs from?* An honest answer to that question was that almost everything I knew about Northern Ireland came from newspapers, journals, radio or television. But my researches of media accuracy in the past suggested to me that these sources might not exactly be the fountainhead of truth. So I decided to do two things immediately: to read all the available literature in *book form* dealing with this problem and to visit Northern Ireland myself and check out as much as possible on the ground.

To cut a long story short I read, in all, almost fifty different books by writers of distinction, Irish, American, British and Continental and the result of this marathon reading was to show me that at least seventy-five per cent of my beliefs concerning Northern Ireland were away off the mark. I cannot say that I found it easy to admit to myself that I had been 'conned' by what seemed a superb propaganda machine that really left Dr Josef Goebbels looking like Little Boy Blue. Later I visited the ghettos in the North and had dozens of interviews with people on both sides of the divide. These visits and interviews, alas, only confirmed my gullibility. Sometimes when a writer feels he has been deceived he slinks away and discreetly forgets, but I am somehow made in the opposite mould. If I had been fooled, I thought, it is possible that thousands, even millions, of others might also have been fooled. It was the very thought of that possibility which spurred me on to write this book.

I then remembered Emerson's famous saying that all history is really biography and so what better interpretation of history could I give than Bobby Sands whom I now saw as a microcosm of the very roots of the whole Northern question as well as being a kind of moral catalyst for the Southern Irish conscience. Twice, with his family, he was intimidated by a Unionist gang and compelled to leave his home and move to other areas. At gunpoint he was ordered to give up his job. Later he was waylaid in the dark and stabbed several times. The police and other forces of law and order, including the Southern politicians, would neither give him help nor protection. What options had he left? He joined the IRA with the object of destroying the system that produced such injustice and of helping to free half-a-million Nationalists from its grip. The story of Bobby Sands is the story of thousands of other young Irish boys and girls in Northern Ireland whose options are almost non-existant. Later he found himself on a world stage watched by millions of people as he confronted and withstood the most powerful forms of pressure, both from Church and State, that could be brought to bear on any human being. In the end he died without yielding and through this terrible death he succeeded in telling the world what British rule in Northern Ireland was really like. In so doing it is possible that he contributed more to the ending of Partition than all the efforts of the previous sixty years. The story of Bobby Sands seemed to me to be the story of Northern Ireland today.

Violence is a word that has been bandied about a lot by speechmakers but it is a reality that has to be faced. The best definition of violence I have been able to find is that of the great South American Archbishop, Dom Helder Camera. Archbishop Camera shows that violence has three different yet indivisible tiers: *The Violence of Injustice, The*

Violence of Reaction and *Institutional Violence*. Serious injustice in any state is in itself a major act of violence. This in turn produces the second tier, the reaction of the oppressed populace to injustice, which in turn produces the third tier, the reaction of security forces to the second tier. It is of course a waste of time trying to eliminate the second and third tiers while the first still exists. Contrarywise eliminate the first tier and you automatically eliminate the other two. So when I speak of violence in this book, I speak of it in the context of these three indivisible dimensions.

As they read through these pages my readers will come to realise that I do not see the majority of politicians in the role of benevolent guardian angels concerned only with the public good. My experience, which gradually grew on me, is that many of them see the right and wrong of a question as totally irrelevant. As I understand it the standards by which most of them judge matters, even matters of life and death, are the acquisition of more votes or more power that will lead to votes. Because of this outlook lying, dishonesty, misrepresentation, evasion, duplicity and double-dealing are part and parcel of their stock-in-trade. When such a politician takes a particular course of action or makes a statement, he does not necessarily do so because he thinks it is right. More likely it is because he considers it tactically sound for the acquisition of more votes or more influence. The majority of politicians firmly believe that they really can fool most of the people all the time and I regret to say history has proved them right.

It is for this reason I have tried to concern myself throughout the book with what is termed *realpolitik*. This is a German word which literally translated means the *policy of reality*. It was widely practised by Bismark and successive German statesmen, and it took the form of always giving priority to real material advantage and not to illusory ideals. Today it could best be expressed by the words *reality politics*. Let me give an example of what I mean.

When the bombs placed recently in London by the IRA killed nine soldiers several public bodies and commercial concerns in Ireland condemned this action and sent emotionally worded messages of sympathy to their counterpart organisations in England. These actions generated a great deal of publicity in the media. However the student of *realpolitik* would question some of the motives behind these expressions of horror and sorrow. He would wonder if all those involved were really concerned with the sentiments they expressed or if material advantage did not play a lurking role. He would be thinking to himself that it might be more truthful and real if those people said: 'We will ignore the fact that your British army in the past few years killed hundreds of innocent Irish men, women and children in Ulster, but we will resoundly condemn the London bombings, because if we don't do something like that your tourists might not come here and this would hurt our pockets very severely.' This attitude might be called cynicism but it is not. In no way does it condone the London bombings — it merely questions some of the motives behind the expression of sympathy. It is *realpolitik*.

Realpolitik is like looking at a television programme from behind the cameras where one sees the props, the lights, the make-up and the entire illusion of what is being foisted on the viewers.

Throughout this book I have tried to apply this yardstick of *realpolitik* to many situations and I regret to say that for the most part I have been unsuccessful. In all matters where the politicians, both British and Irish, have a hand, the layers of deception are so thick that one would need an intellectual bulldozer to move even the top sod. But I do hope I have drawn attention to certain awkward questions which many readers might care to pursue themselves. I do not take any particular pleasure in posing these questions, in lifting stones to see the bloated insects underneath, but I had to do so in order to suggest to readers how they might rescue truth from the rubble of political jargon and deception. Truth is a very splendid thing but one often requires great courage to look it straight in the eye.

If it seems that I have not highlighted the extreme violence of the Nationalist paramilitaries it is solely because it has been so well blazoned and placarded already. What has not been so well publicised is the fact that the majority of acts of violence in Northern Ireland *were the result of institutional violence,* i.e. they were caused, not by the paramilitaries, but by the security forces. It is easy to be negative and to condemn but so difficult to try to understand, to construct, to build on whatever good is around. If there is ever to be peace in Northern Ireland, the ruling classes of both countries will have to sit down and talk with the men of violence. That again is *realpolitik.* Could a beginning not be made now? Could those who in their righteousness condemn, not recall the words of W. B. Yeats:

> Too long a sacrifice
> Can make a stone of the heart?

I need hardly say that I am not a member of any paramilitary organisation, nor indeed of any political party. In writing this book I have tried to discover the truth, but I did not suppress any truth because it happened to favour any paramilitary group. When, on the orders of Michael Collins, the IRA shot Sir Henry Wilson, De Valera was asked if he approved. He replied: 'I do not approve but I cannot pretend not to understand.' Having completed the research necessary for this book that would be my attitude to a lot of what is happening today, and I later learned that it was also the attitude of a large number of responsible thinking people who realise that peace without justice is the perfect recipe for continued violence.

No doubt I will be severely criticised by historians because I have tried to make complicated problems simple and readable and because I have tried to understand the *realpolitik* of situations. They have done that before in their onslaughts on my book *The Shooting of Michael Collins* but I believe I shall have little trouble in surviving their barrages. Criticism is good but to be constructive and honest it must abandon bigotry and prejudice and try to understand. Honest criticism never comes from minds frozen against truth and over the past few years I have learned that Ireland is not entirely free from an intellectual ice age.

In the course of writing this book, I had to talk with,

amongst others, many of the men who are currently being termed 'thugs, murderers and criminals'. I was conditioned to expect a kind of seedy cross between Bill Sykes and Al Capone. The reality turned out to be quite different. Those with whom I spoke were reasonable, intelligent and dedicated young men. They would much prefer to live a normal life but this was denied them and they had come to the end of the road, to the point where they believed that only the gun produced results. Again and again they quizzed me as to what I would personally do if I had been treated as they and their families were. Again and again I funked the answer. Responsible elements within the British army itself privately admitted to admiring their dedication and self-sacrifice while publicly condemning them. There was nothing very secretive about them except their whereabouts. None of them were in the £20,000 a year bracket of most of their public critics. In fact, I doubt if any of them had little more than pocket money. They spoke freely to me and answered my questions, even though with my background they had no reason to trust me too far. In trying to help me many ran great personal risks. At their own request I am respecting their anonymity but despite this they will understand how deeply grateful I am.

It is at this point that many readers might expect me to pose the pompous and self-righteous question: How could such reasonable men carry out the killings they have? I spent fifteen years of my life in the army and I know the mind of a soldier and the way he thinks when a war is on. To those seeking an answer to this question, I suggest that they read any good military biography or indeed any good biography of Michael Collins, Tom Barry or Dan Breen. A soldier with a gun in his hand does not exactly think like a Child of Mary or a Jehovah's Witness. I am not recommending the way of the soldier but I think that *realpolitik* demands that we at least try to understand it.

I would like to express my special gratitude to Gerard Rooney, a close friend of Bobby Sands, for the help he gave me. He is now a prisoner in Portlaoise jail and I would like to thank the then Minister for Justice, Mr Seán

Doherty TD for granting me permission to interview Mr Rooney there, as well indeed as the prison staff who facilitated my visit.

The writing of this book would of course have been almost impossible were it not for the co-operation and kindness of the Sands family: Bobby's parents Rosaleen and John, his sisters Marcella and Bernadette, his brother Seán. They invited me many times to their home and made me feel as if I were an old friend. Conversing in their soft musical Northern accents they spoke freely of Bobby, of his childhood, of his youth, of his ideals, of his suffering and they finally re-lived for me those harrowing days when hour by hour and minute by minute they watched him die. In every sense of the word they gave me their complete confidence and I can truthfully say that I do not recall any time in my life when I have been so greatly honoured. Whenever I think badly of human nature I have only to remember the nobility and dignity of the Sands family to have my faith restored. Bobby was once part of that wonderful family. That is no longer so. He now belongs to the world.

J.M.F.
February 1983

1

The Background

This is not a natural state of any kind at all. It is an artificial product created to destroy political rights and to maintain one group of people in power. By its very essence it denies every principle of democracy.

RICHARD CROSSMAN MP
Labour Cabinet Minister

The man was a publican and a Roman Catholic and was therefore liable to assassination.

NORTHERN IRELAND ATTORNEY-GENERAL,
later LORD CHIEF JUSTICE BABBINGTON

Day after day, week after week, month after month the nation that gave Magna Carta and Habeas Corpus and Due Process to the world imprisons hundreds of innocent citizens of Northern Ireland without warrant, charge or trial, often on the evidence of the rankest hearsay and deception. We read the reports of torture with horror as they describe the efforts of British intelligence to learn the secrets of the IRA by methods no civilised people can countenance.

SENATOR EDWARD KENNEDY

On Thursday 7 May 1981 the people of Belfast witnessed one of the largest funerals ever seen in Ireland since the death of Parnell. It was the funeral of a young Member of Parliament, Bobby Sands — labelled a criminal by Margaret Thatcher — a young poet who died after sixty-six days of a painful hunger-strike and eight years of imprisonment.

A hundred thousand people walked in silence behind the draped coffin and almost as many more lined the route. Old men and young, dazed women and bewildered children cried openly as the coffin holding his ravaged body slowly passed them by. He had died when all earth was bursting into life, when summer was softly creeping over his own Belfast hills, when the larks were soaring high in the sky bringing the music of hope to the weary, war-torn people of this stricken, smouldering city.

Earlier at the Requiem Mass in St Luke's church there was an unpleasant moment when a rule requiring the removal of the Irish flag from the coffin was enforced. It was hard for the onlookers to understand this regulation since they full well knew that had the flag been a Union Jack it would have been permitted. Indeed many would have left the church in disgust were it not for the fact that they did not wish to offend the family. This critical attitude of the crowd was not helped either by the knowledge that, apart from the Funeral Mass, all public Masses for the repose of the soul of Bobby Sands were prohibited. Several priests wanted to concelebrate Mass that day but permission was again refused.

At two o'clock in the afternoon, the tricolour was once more put on the coffin and the funeral set out on the four mile journey to Milltown Cemetery. It was led by a lone piper playing one of the Nationalist songs which begin with the words:

But I'll wear no convict's uniform
Nor meekly serve my time
That Britain's might call Ireland's fight
Eight hundred years of crime.

At Suffolk, the police directed the cortège into the Nationalist Lenadoon estate to avoid going through the small Unionist enclave at Woodburn. Near the Busy Bee Shopping Centre there was a halt and the coffin was temporarily removed from the hearse and rested gently on steel trestles by the open roadway. Then from the midst of the throng there emerged four armed Nationalist paramilitaries who with military precison fired three rifle volleys over the coffin. They then reversed their rifles, bowed their heads and observed a minute's silence before disappearing into the crowd.

When the funeral reached the gates of Milltown Cemetery which holds the graves of hundreds of men, women and children killed by the army, police or Unionists, the sombre crowd burst into spontaneous fervent prayer. A guard of honour accompanied the coffin to the graveside. There the sad, haunting melody of the Last Post rose in spiral sound to echo through the surrounding hills. The family stood by the graveside bowed and tearstained. The perfume from the masses of flowers mingled with that of the rich, fragrant earth as Owen Carron, Bobby Sands' election agent, delivered the graveside oration.

'It is hard to describe the sadness and sorrow in our hearts today,' he said, 'as we stand at the grave of Volunteer Bobby Sands, cruelly murdered by the British government in the H-Block of Long Kesh. . . Bobby has gone to join the ranks of Ireland's patriotic dead. I have no doubt that his name will mark a watershed in Irish history and will be a turning point in the struggle for Irish freedom. . . Indeed Bobby is a hero and I would like first of all to express on behalf of the Republican Movement our sincere sympathy with his family and to pay tribute to them for standing by him courageously to the end. Someone once said it is hard to be a hero's mother and nobody knows that better than Mrs Sands who watched her son being daily crucified and tortured for sixty-six long days and eventually killed. Mrs Sands epitomises the Irish mothers who in every generation watched their children go out to fight and die for freedom. Despite the vilifications and slanders of some guttersnipe media and despite the hypocrisy of high churchmen and establishment politicians who condemned him, Bobby Sands will be remembered by freedom loving people throughout the world. . . His determination and resolve were remarkable and his commitment and dedication total and without compromise. Always in evidence was his sincerity and compassion. . . even his enemies agreed there was no hatred in him. . . Bobby Sands, as representative of the blanket-men and women, died rather than be branded as a criminal. . . The callous intransigence of the British government has made the hunger-strike a symbol of the struggle for freedom. . . Bobby Sands is a symbol of hope for the unemployed, for the poor, for the homeless, for those divided by partition and for those trying to unite our people. . . Bobby Sands has not died in vain. . . He symbolises the true Irish nation which never has surrendered

19

and never will. Let us picture him lying all alone in his cell, his body tortured and twisted in pain, surrounded by his enemies and isolated from his comrades and nothing to fight with but his will and determination. . . The big British murder machine assisted by those in high places in church and state tried to break his spirit. . . They tried to compromise him and his supporters but they failed.'

In a voice filled with emotion Owen Carron concluded:

'Finally, I salute you Bobby Sands. Yours has been a tough, lonely battle but you have been victorious. Your courage and bravery have been an inspiration to us all and today we take strength from your example. Your sacrifice will not be in vain. . .'

The coffin was lowered into the grave. Bobby's father, brother and little son threw in the ritual spadeful of earth. 'Earth to earth, ashes to ashes, dust to dust.' The tricolour was folded and, together with his gloves and beret, presented to his sorrowing mother. Slowly the people left the cemetery and went home with only their memories of yet another victim of war. In their lives the sadness of death was forever replacing the joy of living.

In the quiet evening silence of Milltown graveyard it seemed as if the Republican Movement had reached its Calvary with no Resurrection in sight, that Bobby Sands had lost and the overwhelming power of the British empire had won yet another victory.

But had it? Slowly at first, as if an initial shock had to be surmounted, the protests began. They quickly gathered momentum and in the weeks that followed this tragic day there was scarcely a country in the world that did not in some way commemorate the death of this young Irishman. Although the British propaganda machine got to work with full force, for once it was helpless before the onrush of worldwide sympathy.

In the United States over ten thousand people marched in protest to the British consulates in New York, San Francisco, Boston and Chicago. The state of Rhode Island proclaimed a day of national mourning and the New York state passed a resolution of sympathy and condemned the British. American dockers blacked all British ships on the day of the funeral. A group of influential American senators, including Ted Kennedy, sent an urgent letter to Margaret Thatcher protesting at the 'inflexible posture which must lead inevitably to more senseless violence and death.' 'Surely,' they said, 'the leaders of Great Britain have an urgent responsibility to end this tragic and unnecessary conflict.' But Thatcher, seemingly anxious to prove her manhood, refused.

In Portugal the parliament observed a minute's silence, and in the city of Le Mans, France, a new street was named *Bobby Sands Street*. There were widespread protests in France, Switzerland, West Germany, Belgium, Holland, Norway, Greece, Italy and almost every other European country. In Brisbane, Australia, demonstrators poured mock blood on a British flag and took it to the local offices of the British High Commissioner. But perhaps the most touching message of all came from Lech Walesa who sent his deepest sympathy on behalf of the whole Solidarity movement in Poland.

At home a day of national mourning was observed, despite the official disapproval of the Fianna Fáil government, and in many cities and towns in Ireland shops and businesses closed and thousands of marchers walked in silent protest. This official attitude contrasted strangly with that of previous Fianna Fáil governments. In February 1940 when two IRA men, Peter Barnes and James McCormack, were executed in England for the Coventry bombings, the then Fianna Fáil government declared a day of national mourning and flags were flown at half-mast on all public buildings. And when IRA man Tom Williams was sentenced to death in Belfast in 1942 the same Fianna Fáil government conducted a massive and widespread campaign for his reprieve. This drastic change of attitude is frequently quoted by Nationalists to show that at the time of Bobby Sands' death Fianna Fáil had abandoned its early ideals.

The Fine Gael party had, however, not changed in its cooperative attitude towards Britain. Strict instructions were issued by party headquarters to all their urban and county councillors not to vote for any motion of sympathy when such a motion came before the council. But quite a number of them ignored this rather insensitive direction.

The reaction of the world press was instant, and a lot of it highly critical of the British. Perhaps because of this the London press closed ranks and blazed into an emotive hysteria. The *Daily Telegraph* said: 'No kind of glory attends the suicide of Robert Sands. Courage he had, but it was the courage of the ruthless and corrupted sort which holds human life in contempt.' The *London Times* said: 'The British government bears no responsibility whatever for Mr Sands' death. He committed suicide. . . he was not being oppressed or ill-treated. Indeed the opposite was true.' The *Daily Mail* used the occasion to give its valued opinions on Catholics: '. . . it is one of the alarming characteristics of all too many Catholics these days that they seem ready to excuse terrorism or terrorists where those involved are fellow Catholics.' The *Sun* wrote under the heading SANDS LEGACY OF EVIL: 'It was Bobby Sands who stood for tyranny. . . his hope was that from the grave his twisted sacrifice would impel other men into twisted acts of bloody revenge.' But a real gem came from the *Daily Express:* 'Why then do young men like Robert Sands commit suicide for such a cause? Because they follow darkness, believing it to be a romantic dream. Hatred is their goal. Falsehood is their goal.' The *Daily Mirror* was more restrained: 'Sands died in the Maze in more senses than one. It is not only the name of a prison. It is a description of Irish politics. Britain has been trapped in that maze for too long. Its task now is to find the way which will lead it out altogether.'

Reaction of the foreign press was somewhat different. The *New York Daily News* said: 'He was a rare one, a young man who thought enough of the place where he lives to want to die for it.' Spain's *El Païs* condemned Britain's implacable toughness. West Germany's *Allegemeine Zeitung* said that 'The death of Bobby Sands turned attention to the weak point of British democracy.' In France *Le Monde* said: 'His memory and recognition of the meaning of his sacrifice are heavy with an emotion that several times this century has aroused the passions of the world against Britain.' The *Hindustan Times* said that Thatcher 'had allowed a member of the House of Commons, a colleague in fact, to die of starvation. Never had such an incident occurred in a civilised country.'

At home the reaction was intriguing. The Unionist *Belfast Telegraph* said: 'It is difficult for any Irish Nationalist to accept that the British government may be in the right. . .' The *Irish Times* carried a special supplement on Bobby Sands and concluded: 'Governments. . . must know when to temper the rules of law with understanding, sympathy, mercy. . . the British government could not rise to this.' The *Irish Press* said: 'Belfast narrowed his options as a boy, gunmen chased him from his home and from his job. . . In jail Britain narrowed his options to two: live as a criminal or die for an ideal. His choice will be long remembered. . . Mrs Thatcher is institutionalising brutality in her prison in the H-Block and guaranteeing, not merely risking, massive violence and bloodshed on the streets of Northern Ireland.'

This extraordinary world press coverage, of which this is but a tiny section, was supplemented, and one might say, reinforced by an equally massive radio and television coverage and indeed it is now generally believed that more people saw the funeral of Bobby Sands on their screens than saw the year's most publicised event, the royal wedding.

No matter how one looks at it, or what one's politics are, one is compelled to ask the question: Do responsible statesmen, parliaments, newspapers, journalists, television presenters in every country in the world sympathetically and favourably comment upon convicted 'criminals' such as Mrs Thatcher described Bobby Sands? Is there any single case in the entire history of the world where the death of a 'criminal' was accorded such international admiration and sympathy?

His friend and comrade Danny Morrison paid a last moving tribute after the British refused him permission to say farewell:

> My dear friend and comrade, although it has happened I still can't believe it. I would have liked to have said good-bye and shook that rare strong hand once more, but that was denied me. You are at peace now, out of the hell blocks that murdered you, out of the clutches of the screws and of British rule, like the lark, free and at peace. Now we need your prayers, your courage and determination, that beautiful unvanquished spirit that brought you through those tribulations. Watch over us.

To understand the world into which Bobby Sands was born we must take a brief look at the conditions which existed in the six counties of Ulster, commonly referred to as Northern Ireland, since its establishment after the Treaty. Human beings are moulded and developed not only by parental and home influences but also by the influences of the political, social and economic milieu surrounding them. This milieu had a decisive impact on the short life of Bobby Sands.

The Six County State had its origins in the seventeenth century when, after the defeat of the native Irish chieftains, the British occupation forces evicted hundreds of thousands of Irish Catholics from their lands and homes and replaced them with English and Scottish Protestants. The present Unionists in the North are the descendants of these settlers. But they have long since ceased to be an ethnic group. There were many other parts of Ireland where the British dispossessed the Irish and gave their land to foreigners, but the largest concentration was in the northern part of the country where they were numerically strong enough to form a pressure group of almost coercive power. Those of the dispossessed Irish who remained at home and did not emigrate became the hewers of wood and drawers of water, menial servants in their own country, subservient to their dispossessors. The present Nationalists are descended from these dispossessed Irish.

The French Revolution spread ideas of freedom and equality which were highly odious in the eyes of these settlers, particularly as some of their own class were affected by them, and so they banded themselves, with the approval of the British government, into an extreme sectarian organisation known as the Orange Order to ensure absolute and uncompromising dominance over their confiscated territory. This organisation might be described as the Klu-Klux-Klan of Ireland and was, through intimidation, imprisonment and bloodshed to dominate all aspects of life in Northern Ireland down to the present day.

Because of its discipline, its tightness, its offer of security, the Orange Order succeeded in stripping its members of all individuality and substituting therefor the mind and philosophy of its leaders. It became a vast political machine involving thousands of minions who had a personal interest in seeing that all decisions concerning jobs, housing, welfare, education and public affairs in general conformed to the overall designs and plans of its bosses. Its great weapon was hatred. With consummate skill it succeeded in inculcating into its members a fanatical, venomous, inflammable hatred of everything and everyone Irish. Mainly by this weapon it created in Northern Ireland a statelet where virtually all who did not support the Orange Order were dehumanised. Sadly and surprisingly to some, Britain, mother of democracies, supported and financed this artificial state.

No doubt the British government had its own reasons for giving its full support to the Orange Order. They were only putting into effect their old formula 'divide and conquer'. A divided and disunited Ireland posed little threat to Britain and could be reasonably kept in line and subjected if it were really necessary by a crack of the whip. British Chief Secretary Sir Robert Peel put it in a nutshell: 'I hope they may always be disunited. The great art is to keep them so.'

In 1921 when Britain sued for peace in the war between

the IRA and the British army, Ireland was given a measure of freedom roughly corresponding to the kind of dominion status enjoyed by Canada and Australia. But this independence excluded an undefined area in Northern Ireland where the Unionists, as the adherents of the Orange Order called themselves, had a majority. Michael Collins had agreed privately with Lloyd George that this area would not exceed three, or at the very most, four of the Ulster counties. This was later confirmed by both Churchill and Lloyd George to Tim Healy MP. Collins was satisfied that the small Northern statelet of three or four counties only, would become an unviable economic unit and would eventually unite with the rest of the country. Practically alone among the Irish political leaders of the time Collins was the one with a real effective concern for the Nationalists of the North. 'No matter what happens,' he told them publicly, 'no matter what the future may bring, we shall not desert you.' He never went back on that promise. When things got bad in the North he sent large consignments of arms and ammunition to help the Nationalists, and when the brutality of Sir Henry Wilson, the Unionists' military adviser, resulted in the killing of scores of Nationalists Collins had him shot.

Later when Collins was killed under most mysterious circumstances his successors in the new Free State government of the South, seemingly anxious to be good members of the British Commonwealth handed over *six* counties without too much persuasion. It is interesting to note here that the original idea of the Orange Order was to take over all *nine* counties of Ulster. However, when the Unionists did their sums, they found that the Nationalist majority in all *nine* counties of Ulster would be too great to manipulate, so they chose only *six* counties which would prove much easier to gerrymander and dominate. The inclusion of the three other counties, Donegal, Cavan and Monaghan, would in the words of Sir James Craig, first premier of the Six Counties, 'Reduce our majority to such a level that no sane man could carry on Parliament with it.' This must be the only case in the history of the world where a new state refused extra rich and prosperous territory which could be had for the asking. It was in this unusual but calculated way the state of Northern Ireland, based entirely on a privileged class, came into being.

One important aspect of the creation of the Six-County State was that De Valera and the deputies loyal to him could have thrown a spanner in the works but chose not to do so. Because of the compulsory oath of allegiance to the British king he and his fellow deputies refused to enter the new Irish parliament, Dáil Éireann. The creation of the Six-County statelet required the agreement of the Dáil and quite a few of the government deputies disagreed with their leader and together with Labour and Independent deputies they approached De Valera with the proposal that they would dissent and vote against the bill. Together with De Valera's deputies they would have constituted a majority and could thus defeat the bill. They suggested that he and his followers enter the Dáil, even if it were for one day only. This proposal was refused and so the Six-County state came legally into being. A few years later De Valera did an about turn, took the oath and entered the Dáil. Why he did not do so earlier, and so have struck a blow against the forcible alienation of the Nationalists in the North and perhaps saved countless thousands of lives since, is still a mystery.

Around forty per cent of the population of this new statelet are Nationalists who did not want to have any hand, act or part of it but they were forced against their will, on the one hand by the British and on the other by the new Irish government in the South. This is a most important factor in the understanding of the present war in the North, and of why the Nationalists have resorted to force. The Nationalist population of the Six Counties want to join up with and be part of the southern Republic but successive southern governments have cold-shouldered them in such a way as to make them feel unwanted. Again and again throughout this book this sad point will crop up: *Oratory apart, there is no evidence whatever to show that either of the main political parties in the South want an independent united Ireland.* This unfortunately is *realpolitik.* In the allotment of blame for the present violence in Northern Ireland successive Southern governments must surely bear a heavy burden of responsibility which speechmaking cannot easily conceal.

In the new Six-County realm the Orange Order set about consolidating their position by creating what was virtually a police state. Their first step was to gerrymander the constituency boundaries to ensure the almost total disenfranchisement of the Nationalist minority. The population of the Six Counties was approximately sixty per cent Unionist and forty per cent Nationalist so that on this basis out of eighty-two local councils the Nationalists should have controlled about thirty and the Unionists fifty. But so well was the job of gerrymandering accomplished by Sir John Leech KC that the Unionists controlled eighty councils and the Nationalists only two. The Unionist Chief Whip, Major L. E. Curran made no bones about it: 'The best way to prevent the overthrow of the government by people who had no stake in the country and had not the welfare of the people of Ulster at heart was to disenfranchise them.' There was uproar from the few opposition deputies at this statement. The Unionists now realised that Curran had gone too far and they had this statement discreetly removed from Hansard, the official parliamentary reports, when it was being printed. Whatever official did this piece of 'censorship' bungled the job by deleting Curran's statement and leaving in all the attacks made on him by the opposition!

This kind of disenfranchisement continued throughout the Six Counties leaving the Nationalist population with no voice whatever in the running of the state. County Fermanagh is a particularly interesting case. Mr E. C. Ferguson, Unionist MP for Enniskillen said: 'The Nationalist majority in Co. Fermanagh, notwithstanding a reduction of 336 in this year, stands at 3,604. I would ask the meeting to authorise their executive to take whatever steps, however drastic, to liquidate this Nationalist majority.' Apparently the necessary steps were taken. Even though the

Nationalists have a fifty-one per cent population majority here they were only able to get seventeen seats on the council as against the Unionists' thirty-six.

This devilish job of gerrymandering gave them virtually complete control over all state and semi-state employment. They used this predominance to the maximum and with great success. Of all government jobs ninety per cent were filled by Unionists. Those few jobs that went to the Nationalists were usually menial clerkships. Now and again a moderately important job would be given to a non-Unionist so that if any adverse comment came, say from Britain, they were able to point to this appointment as camouflage. One cabinet minister, however, Sir Dawson Bates, had such a hatred of Nationalists that he made it clear to his senior civil servants that not even the most junior clerk in his ministry was to be employed if he were a Nationalist. In one purge Sir Basil Brooke, later Lord Brookeborough, sacked one hundred and twenty-five employees when he found out they were Nationalists. His exact words were: 'If we in Ulster allow Roman Catholics to work on our farms we are traitors to Ulster.' When he publicly urged all employers not to give work to Nationalists there was an outcry, but the prime minister, Lord Craigavon, backed him up fully. 'There is not one of my colleagues who does not entirely agree with him,' he said, 'and I would not ask him to withdraw one word.'

Since virtually all private industry was in the hands of members of the Orange Order the same pattern applied. There were very few jobs for Nationalists. One employer said publicly that in fifty years his firm had only one Nationalist employee, and that was a case of mistaken identity. In the great shipyard of Harland and Wolff out of ten thousand workers there were only about three hundred Nationalists, and they were given only the lowest pay and most menial jobs. Again in the county of Fermanagh, where there is a Nationalist majority, only three of the seventy-four school busmen employed by the Education Committee were Nationalists. Sadly in 1983, under direct British rule the situation has changed very little.

Another important step in the control of Northern Ireland by the Unionists was the formation of the police force. But first they passed the Civil Authorities (Special Powers) Act 1922. This act gave the police amazing powers of search, arrest, detention, imprisonment without trial, suspension of inquests, prohibition of meetings, burning of publications, confiscation of property, flogging of prisoners. In this Act Regulation 22B says that a person shall not be excused for not answering any question on the ground that the answer may incriminate him. It was of that act that John Vorster, prime minister of South Africa, said he would willingly swap all his anti-communist powers for this one law. This appalling Act was later replaced and strengthened by the Northern Ireland Emergency Provisions Act 1973, consolidated in 1978 and was described by a British Civil Liberties Commission as 'contrary to the fundamental principles of democratic government.' But it still remains in force and as I write these lines it is being daily put into effect, with the full approval of the British government.

This police force is almost entirely Unionist, and since its formation it has operated with a brutal efficiency which can again only be compared to that of the Gestapo or the South African secret police. Torture and even murder have been its most common weapons. Night after night these armed police raided Nationalist houses, dragged men and women and children out of their beds, kicked and beat them up, smashed furniture, pictures and family heirlooms. And there was no redress. The highly respected *Manchester Guardian* said:

> The Unionists have an important ally. They have a coercive police force of their own. . . They have become the instruments of religious tyranny. . . parading their districts at night with arms, harassing, threatening, beating and occasionally killing their Catholic neighbours and burning their homes.

The following terrible statistics speak for themselves. In 1971 there were 17,292 raids on Nationalists' homes. In 1972 this had risen to 36,614 and in 1974 had risen again to

71,914. *This is approximately two hundred houses raided per day.* And the RUC now have the British army to help them on these raids, as well as intelligence from the police in Southern Ireland.

Perhaps worst of all were the auxiliary police force known as the 'B Specials'. They were an exclusively Unionist sectarian force who were allowed to keep arms and weapons in their homes and who actually participated in ruthless and gruesome pogroms against Nationalists. In the dark of the night, aided by Unionist paramilitaries, they attacked Nationalist areas, burned houses, indeed sometimes whole streets, evicted the old, the poor, the sick, women and children and rendered them completely homeless. It is estimated that sixty thousand people were thus driven from their homes, and in Milltown Cemetery alone there are close on one thousand graves of men, women and children killed during these pogroms.

Well might the respected *Manchester Guardian* again comment:

> Whilst envenomed politicians in the Ulster parliament are voting themselves power to use torture and capital punishment against citizens whom they forbid to defend themselves while they scarcely attempt to protect them from massacre, some of their own partisans in Belfast carry wholesale murder to refinements of barbarity hardly surpassed in Armenia and Constantinople.'

This terrible regime had the backing of the British government who in the 'thirties and early 'forties were condemning a similar regime in Germany, but ignoring it within their own jurisdiction. The Nationalist population had nowhere to turn. Plea after plea to the British fell on deaf ears. But far worse still was the fact that similar heart-rending pleas for help to the Southern Ireland government were rejected too. W. T. Cosgrave, Eamon de Valera, Seán Lemass, or any other Irish prime minister never took any real effective steps to help their suffering, persecuted brethren in the North. This is a hard, cold, unpalatable *realpolitik* truth which we will run up against again and again. These politicians did not seem to want a united Ireland that would upset the rule of party politics in Dáil Éireann. They were quite prepared to make grandiloquent, verbose and stirring speeches, but everything ended with the last full stop.

Most of these unfortunate people were Catholics but again the leaders of their Church did little of practical value to help them. They did not openly side with the Unionists and they certainly disapproved of much of what the Unionists were doing, but they confined their activities to speechmaking, and to sermons advising their flock to turn the other cheek.

The leaders of all the Protestant Churches made no protest of any kind but on the contrary they fully acquiesced in the injustices of the Unionist regime. It is therefore little wonder that the Nationalists of today treat with searing cynicism the orations of these gentlemen after fifty years of silence.

This was the society into which Bobby Sands was born. Unlike most young people in any civilised country he could not look forward to a happy childhood or a normal fulfilled manhood. His role was predetermined among the besieged people with whom he lived. It was the role of a doormat, of servility, persecution and suffering and there was little brightness on the horizon.

For fifty years his besieged people had tried every peaceful means to improve their lot, to eke out even a hand-to-mouth existence but they were met only by brutality and repression from the Unionist government, contempt from the British, apathy from the Irish government and Irish politicians and indifference from their Church. They felt themselves isolated and alone.

Two stark unpalatable truths stared them in the face. Firstly, they saw they would have to help themselves. No one would take any real practical steps to help them. Secondly, it became painfully clear that little would be achieved by peaceful means. They had tried and failed and now they saw their only hope in violence. So skilfully has the brainwashing of the public been carried out that only the thoughtful minority have seen the unpalatable fact that violence was the last resort of a people beaten almost into insensitivity.

By way of a final word to end this chapter should we not look back at Archbishop Camera's three tiers of violence and honestly ask the *realpolitik* question: Who are those responsible for the first tier, the violence of injustice? A still more embarrassing question might be: What Irish politicians are today publicly condemning those responsible?

Fifty years of suffering and oppression had exhausted the patience of the minority, hardened their spirits and put iron into their souls. In 1969 they took to the streets in their thousands armed only with sticks and stones. The reign of violence had begun.

2

Caveat Emptor

The victor will never be asked if he told the truth.

ADOLF HITLER

Truth is so precious that we must protect it with a body-guard of lies.

WINSTON CHURCHILL

What happened at Aldershot, what happened at the Old Bailey reminds us that what happens in Londonderry is very relevant to what can happen in London and if we lose in Belfast we may have to fight in Brixton or Birmingham.

JOHN BIGGS DAVIDSON MP
RUSI Seminar 1973

There are many who now believe that the year 1969 was for a large section of the Nationalist people of the Six Counties what 1916 was for the people of the South. They see it as the year when they abandoned non-violence and took to other means in earnest as the only way of achieving even the rudiments of justice.

Before, however, we take a look at the beginning of these momentous events and of Bobby Sands' involvement it might be well to pause and examine broadly some of the uncertainties and inaccuracies in circulation which, if not understood, might easily distort our picture of the man himself and the motives behind his activities. Most of these distortions are the result of a superb British propaganda exercise aided, perhaps unwittingly, by a number of Irish politicians and by sections of the Irish media.

Number One: The public outside Northern Ireland, and particularly in the South, are well and truly informed about what is happening there.

To assess the accuracy of this statement is not too hard.

My own view as I have mentioned in the Introduction is that about seventy per cent of the news portrayed through the media is either inaccurate, incomplete or false. Let me give a few examples of what I mean.

Some time ago Fr Denis Faul, who has written books highly critical of the British, made a strong statement condemning the Provisional IRA. These statements were given the widest publicity in all newspapers, radio and television. Later Fr Faul severely criticised the RUC for their widespread misuse of the Terror Act. He said:

> It is a serious misuse of the Act and the section because men who are held under it are held on an uncorroborated verbal statement in many cases, and some are being blackmailed into giving information. I know of one man from the Divis area who is arrested every fortnight and threatened by police officers that if he does not provide information he will be charged. The man has consistently refused to do this, and is regularly arrested to keep pressure on him.

One would imagine that such a serious statement made by a responsible clergyman would receive wide publicity, at least as much as his anti-IRA statement had. But this is not what happened. Practically all newspapers as well as radio and television ignored him, with the result that few people were made aware of these criticisms of the activities of the RUC.

The shooting by the IRA of a young man in south Armagh as an informer provides another interesting example. The RUC vehemently denied that he was an informer and projected the image on the media that this was just another blood-thirsty IRA murder. Again this statement by the RUC was given wide publicity on radio, television and newspapers. What was *not* given the same publicity was the statement issued by the Republican Press Centre in Belfast. This statement gave the actual dates on which this young man was interrogated by the RUC at Gough Barracks, Armagh. After three days of interrogation he broke down and agreed to act as an informer. He was offered £200 for every IRA rifle to which he led the RUC. In an unmarked van he brought police officers and SAS men to where he believed there was an IRA dump. He also gave the names of a large number of 'safe' houses in the area. He was given the code name 'Peter' and told to ring a number in Dungannon with information. He agreed to set up three leading Republicans for arrest. His contacts at that number were 'Sid' and 'Angela'. He was tried by IRA court-martial and given every chance to defend himself. He was found guilty and shot.

Whatever one's moral judgment on such activities may be at least the public are entitled to expect *all* the facts from the media and not merely one version only.

Last year I myself attended a public lecture by a prominent politician in which he criticised the Provisional IRA, the UDA, the RUC, the British army and Mrs Thatcher. That night on television news only his criticism of the IRA was mentioned and the following day the bulk of the newspapers featured a headline PROMINENT SPEAKER CONDEMNS IRA, without reference to his other condemnations. This is surely one-sided reportage, and unfair to the public.

One of the main objectives of the British is to portray the IRA as thugs and murderers with a lust for blood and in this objective they have been extraordinarily successful particularly in Southern Ireland. It seems therefore a great pity that the following statement issued by the Provisional IRA was not given the publicity that would enable the Irish people to weigh up for themselves if in fact they were thugs and murderers. This important statement was issued as early as 1973:

> Will talk achieve more than the gun? Yes, definitely yes. And the IRA are more than willing to talk. We have said many times that we detest this war with its suffering and misery and we speak from first hand knowledge of that suffering and misery. We would much rather settle our differences in a civilised way. But let one point be very clear. It is the British, not we, who still refuse to negotiate.

In 1981 there was scarcely a media outlet that did not highlight Danny Morrison's famous speech about the 'armalite and the ballot box'. What was never highlighted, however, were other words he uttered:

> We are a peaceful people. I repeat we are a peaceful
> people. But it needs to be said fearlessly, because it is the
> truth: after what we have come through for fifty years, the
> repression, the discrimination. . . it's no crime and there's
> no moral wrong in lifting a stone, planting a bomb, raising a
> rifle against those who oppress our people.

One may agree or disagree with these statements. But
surely the public are entitled to know that such statements
were made. They should not be kept in the dark.

Again we have never been told that five hundred
Nationalist pubs have been blown up, thirty bombing
attacks on Catholic churches and forty thousand
Nationalists bombed and burned out of their homes. The
public are entitled to know of these happenings because
they have a very direct bearing on the motives of Bobby
Sands and other young men like him.

One final example may be quoted. It will be recalled that
a great peace movement was started by Betty Williams and
Mairead Corrigan as a result of the killing of three Maguire
children. The British version of this story is that the
children were killed by a runaway car driven by IRA man
Danny Lennon. But there is another version which was
published on the Continent which says that Danny Lennon
was already dead when the car went out of control. According to what the mother of the dead children, the late Mrs
Maguire, told relatives of Danny Lennon and lawyers from
the Association for Legal Justice, the children had already
been killed by bullets from an SLR British army rifle before
being run down. The results of the post-mortems on these
three children have not been made public. The children's
mother is reported to have said: 'My children also were
killed by the British army and that's why the conclusions of
the forensic specialists will never be made public.'

Surely we are entitled to be given the full facts of this incident whatever these facts are or whichever version is the
correct one. It is simply hoodwinking the public to give the
British version only.

I have given these few examples, out of literally

thousands I have come across, of how vitally important news concerning Northern Ireland does not get over to the public and it is hard to see how such a public could make any kind of a reasoned judgment on the tragic affairs across the border when they are kept in the dark about such important matters. But do those who purvey this news really want us to make a reasoned judgment?

It is my own experience that scarcely a day passes when some item of news concerning Northern Ireland is, by the time it reaches the public, twisted and distorted so as to give the British angle. Not only hundreds but several thousands of such new items favourable to the British point of view have been successfully foisted on the public in Southern Ireland and the cumulative effect of this is that the British army and the RUC are seen as men of honour and nobility, striving to do justice and being prevented from doing so by thugs and gangsters. My advice to anyone who wishes to find out the truth is to go up to the North, particularly Belfast, and just have a look around the Nationalist ghettos. It is an experience that will sharpen the wits and make one quite cautious about accepting what appears in the media. It is also an experience that will tear at the heart strings as few other experiences can.

The British propaganda performance in Southern Ireland has been one of their most outstanding successes but like so many other aspects of the Northern Ireland story it would require a complete book in itself to do any kind of justice to the operation as a whole. Here I can only touch on a few of the skilful techniques which are generally believed to be employed in putting the British point of view.

British propaganda is directed from a press office near Lisburn which is said to have a staff of forty press officers helped by a back-up staff of one hundred and fifty people. Very early on in the troubles they were given the task of moulding opinion in Southern Ireland so that the population would see the Northern problem through British eyes. The planning behind the manoeuvre lay in the belief that if public opinion south of the border could be swung in favour of the British then the politicians would follow suit and the government could thereby be easily nudged into a position of full co-operation with the RUC, the SAS and the army. In this they succeeded beyond their wildest dreams. After one meeting with Charlie Haughey Margaret Thatcher declared: '. . . increasingly we are getting determined and effective co-operation.' Nationalists in the North find it very hard to understand this cross-border co-operation. More than once it was pointed out to me that it would be difficult to imagine, say West Germany, sentencing their citizens on the word of the KGB or the East German Secret Police, or maintaining radio and police links with these police in order to capture East Germans crossing the Berlin Wall. Can anyone imagine Spain co-operating with Britain in this field over Gibraltar?

One British politician said to me: 'Think of what we have achieved. Ten years ago you burned down our embassy in Dublin, most of your population hated us. Now we have you eating out of our hands and your government doing our bidding. Once we have defeated the IRA, with your help, we can get back to the old Stormont days!'

One element not often averted to which has helped the British immensely in their propaganda effort is the natural toadyism of the Irish, particularly in the South. This has a historical basis. For hundreds of years the Irish were treated as slaves in their own country and consequently developed a subconscious slave mentality which is still thriving. In order to survive they had to fawn and cringe before their British masters. Psychologists tell us that there are deep rooted elements in us all known as 'race memories' and that after hundreds of years of a particular way of life the mentality produced by that way of life persists even when the original cause is no longer there. It is as if one planted a sally sapling, tied the top with a rope to the ground so as to form a partial circle and then after twenty years growth cut the rope. The tree would not immediately spring into an upright position. It would take many years of slow movement before it became vertical again, if ever. The Irish are like that tree. They are still on their knees making obeisance before their overlords. Time and again I recall Commandant Tom Barry, the guerrilla leader, speaking of his difficulty in getting some of his men to fire on the British. It seemed as if they developed a mental block when it came to attacking their lords and masters. This toadyism expresses itself in many ways today. Our media will very often give exposure to an Englishman for some work or achievement when at the same time far superior achievements by Irishmen in the same field are ignored. Our politicians are thrilled if some of the British aristocracy condescend to notice them. Our civil servants and police are equally subservient to their counterparts, particularly if they have a title. Many of our public representatives feel deeply honoured to promulgate the British line on the North. It may take another fifty or a hundred years before we can stand on our own feet and remember that our ancestors were bringing culture and civilised living to Europe when Britain was still a very primitive society. Nevertheless this toadyism has made the task of moulding our opinions to the British viewpoint much easier.

Psy-ops (Psychological Operations) is the name given to this operation whereby public opinion is moulded. Its object is to plant pro-British news stories and distorted truths on unsuspecting journalists in all branches of the media. It is carried out with extraordinary skill in so far as it is not recognised for what it really is; its real source is disguised thus giving it the seal of impartiality. A hard-working, hard pressed journalist would suspect a release from the British press office, but would not suspect an outside source or a special news service. It is through such outside sources that psy-ops work, so that a journalist trying to meet a deadline has no cause to suspect when the story comes from what he thinks is an independent agency. One story that psy-ops successfully projected was that the IRA 'godfathers' forced Bobby Sands to remain on hunger-strike. The projection was done when they saw public sympathy swinging in Sands' direction. So successfully did they plant this story that prominent Irish politicians believed it and many of them enunciated it publicly. It is now known and there is

documentary evidence to show that the Republican leadership did everything possible to get Sands and the others off
the hunger-strike but they refused.

Here it might be no harm to mention briefly the role of
the British Secret Service in moulding public opinion in Ireland. When most of us speak of the Secret Service we have
visions of a James Bond-like figure experiencing hair-
raising adventures and admired by a host of exotic women.
The reality is much more mundane. Agents are usually
hard-working men and women with little glamour in their
lives, even if they supplement their incomes from a tax-free
fund. An author of international repute is at present com-
pleting a book on the activities of the British Secret Service
in Ireland and this book will suggest that one cannot rule
out the possibility that part-time British agents are working
in various branches of the media, and indeed in the public
services in positions of importance that would enable them
to slant matters significantly in favour of Britain. I do not
think I am being sensational if I suggest that we keep an
open and enquiring mind and that we study all news and
commentaries put before us with the greatest caution and
vigilance.

Be that as it may I can only say that in the South I have
spoken at length with all classes of people, even those in the
highest of places, and I am constantly astonished at how
seriously misinformed they are about what is happening in
the North. In publishing the *whole truth* and in resisting any
attempts to slant, either from within or without, the media
have an important and very responsible role to play. The
lives of hundreds if not thousands of people may rest in
their hands.

*Number Two: The struggle in Northern Ireland is a Religi-
ous Struggle.*

This statement is an over-simplification and I think that
most people now realise that the conflict has very little to
do with religion. Catholics are not fighting Protestants and
vice versa, simply on the grounds of religion. The conflict
in Northern Ireland is basically between two groups of

people, the Privileged and the Underprivileged, the Haves and the Have-nots. It is an economic conflict. The Privileged are the Orange Order, their minions and supporters, the Underprivileged are the rest of the population. The Orange Order are the overlords — everyone else is the underling. But behind all one suspects the sinister hand of Britain keeping the statelet divided.

The Orange Order control and dominate overwhelmingly the finance, housing, industry, civil service, police, judiciary and all public services. They have in fact most of the 'goodies' for the giving. In a united Ireland, or even in a devolved government with power sharing, they would lose control and would have to compete openly like every other citizen for their share of the national product. They have had sixty years of monopoly and they do not want any change. They say they are loyal to Britain but could it be that their loyalty is only because Britain has backed them fully with her army, navy and police? If the Irish Republic, or indeed the Soviet Union, were effectively to guarantee their monopoly, would they become republicans or communists overnight? I think it is not being too harsh to say that they have little loyalty to crown or constitution — they have only a loyalty to themselves and to their class. Indeed in 1912 the Orange Order were openly discussing that the Kaiser should be invited over to save them from Home Rule!

The majority of the Orange Order are not even practising Protestants, but from every platform they keep up a veritable barrage of sectarian hatred which is so bizzare that it is difficult to believe. They whip up the Protestant working class to a frenzy by telling them that the Catholics will burn them alive, roast them in oil, take their homes and jobs. Unfortunately many simpler Protestants believe this rubbish and they can easily be incited to invade Catholic areas burning, looting, killing in the false belief that they are protecting themselves. This monster of hate is now so entrenched that even if the Unionists wanted to moderate their policies it is doubtful if they could do so in the face of the embedded views of the rank and file.

The nearest equivalent to the Orange Order is the Klu-Klux-Klan in the United States. The KKK persecute Catholics, Jews, Blacks and other ethnic groups. The Orange Order persecute Catholics only because there is no other minority group to threaten them, and they persecute them not on religious grounds but on economic ones. To maintain their privileged position they must ensure that there will *never* be a Nationalist majority. This is what the conflict in Northern Ireland is about, and we will see later on how severely Bobby Sands and his family suffered from this sectarianism.

One of the great myths of British propaganda is that in Ireland there are *two nations*. There are not two nations. There is one nation only, with different traditions. They say, with tongue in cheek, that because the Northern Unionists want to remain with Britain therefore it is a separate nation. The British know quite well that there is only one nation with a privileged group in occupation of one part of it — and they support that group for their own interests. There are of course two traditions in the North and to this one can only say 'So what?' There are three traditions in the Republic, the Gaelic, the Irish and the Anglo-Irish. In Switzerland, Belgium, France, the United States and other countries there are several different traditions. The existence of different traditions in a country does not mean that each tradition must have its own political independence. The Bavarian Catholics can co-exist side by side with Prussian Protestants. In all these countries the various traditions are able to live and work in harmony, but the desire of one tradition to be overlord and to have all the goodies is the reason why the two traditions in Northern Ireland cannot work together. The politically immature speeches of some Southern Irish politicians that we must make fundamental changes in our constitution is an example of the pathetic grasp these politicians have of the whole Northern question. If we turned our constitution upside down and inside out it would not make the slightest difference. The Unionists want to hold on to their privileged position, their total domination of all aspects of life, and they have already treated with utter contempt any suggestion of changes in our constitution.

There is now a possibility that the Nationalists may soon outnumber them but Harold McCusker, Unionist MP recently made it clear that even in such an event they would not accept a United Ireland. Majority rule for Unionists only operates when it suits themselves.

The Unionist struggle in Northern Ireland is about 'goodies' and not about 'gods'.

Number Three: The British want to get out of Northern Ireland. They've had enough.

There are two views about this statement. One says it is true and that they are in Northern Ireland only because they created the state and they feel a sense of loyalty to its citizens and they will leave when the majority so desire. Another view treats this idea with scepticism if not with outright derisive laughter. According to the second view the track-record of Britain occupying countries for reasons of honour and then leaving when requested to do so is not very impressive.

At the present moment the British occupation of Northern Ireland is costing them at least one thousand million pounds per annum. Are they spending that kind of money to impress the world with their honourable intentions? Are they approaching the people of Northern Ireland with an olive branch in one hand and Dale Carnegie's *How to Win Friends and Influence People* in the other? There is quite a body of responsible opinion which holds that Northern Ireland is vital to their entire defence system and they have no intention of withdrawing from there. Not only that, but they regard Southern Ireland also as of major importance to that same defence system.

To examine the details of the present world military situation is not within the scope of this book. I can therefore touch only on a few points which have a particular relevance to the view that Ireland is vital to Britain's defence.

With the constant improvement in weapons of war

Britain can now no longer depend on European countries such as France, Germany, Denmark, Holland, Norway and Sweden to act as a bulwark against a Russian attack. The new Russian cruise missiles with nuclear warheads can be launched from submarines out in the Atlantic Ocean, and fly in across Ireland and devastate practically all the cities of Britain in a matter of minutes. Her very survival, therefore, could depend on her having along the coasts of Ireland a series of laser bases from which such missiles could be effectively destroyed in flight. Instead, therefore, of letting go of Northern Ireland Britain is in fact tightening her grip there, and at the same time gradually pressurising Southern Ireland into some kind of military alliance where the British army will have bases along our coasts. At the present moment the British have twenty defence sites in Northern Ireland against missiles. These sites have been made mobile so that they can be quickly moved to the South if necessary.

What the actual realities of this moment are would be hard to say but at least it behoves us to keep an open mind on the matter especially in view of a statement made some time ago by Humphrey Atkins, former Secretary of State for Northern Ireland. He said: 'Sixty years ago Britain and Ireland — a lot of Ireland — got separated. *I think we can reverse that.' (Italics mine)*. This is a rather startling statement from a top British cabinet minister who was never officially contradicted by any member of the Irish government. Again in an important interview in the *Sunday Tribune* Mr Seán MacBride, Nobel peace prizewinner, claimed that senior officials of the Department of Foreign Affairs are determined to end Irish neutrality and bring us into a West European defence alliance. This has not been publicly contradicted by any responsible government official. Neither has there been any official comment on an editorial in the well-informed *Guardian* which said: '. . . it is more generally acknowledged in Dublin than is often realised that these two islands cannot be thought of as entirely separate units.'

Finally the new Irish high-capacity micro-wave communications system now being set up in Ireland envisages the closest links with Britain. An excellent article in *In Dublin* magazine, 6 August 1982, by Brendan Munnelly on the forms of co-operation in operation, and envisaged, in the field of communications between Ireland and Britain and unknown to the Irish public makes uneasy and disquieting reading. So whatever actually is afoot between the two countries, most thinking Irish people could not be blamed for having considerable doubt about Britain's real intentions. I do not feel I am being an alarmist if I suggest that we should all keep a vigilant, sharp eye on these matters.

Number Four: The Political Parties in the South want a United Ireland under a single government in Dublin.

There is no solid concrete evidence to show that any of the main Southern political parties really want a united Ireland under a single government in Dublin. I use the words 'solid' and 'concrete' specifically to distinguish between something real and practical and not something contained in a speech. In any view of Northern Ireland one must clearly distinguish between the verbosity of politicians, ecclesiastics and others and the actual reality of what they are prepared to do. The evidence I am unable to find concerns real, positive, practical action. Such evidence is virtually non-existent and it is not unreasonable to conclude that these political parties are not really serious about a united Irish Republic.

The old Fine Gael party (Cumann na nGaedheal) were horrified at the republicanism of Michael Collins and at his readiness to use force against the North, so they skilfully had him removed as head of the Irish Provisional Government and stripped of cabinet rank just before he was mysteriously shot. They then dedicated themselves to becoming good, obedient and loyal members of the British Commonwealth. In 1925 having withdrawn from the Boundary Commission they handed over the six Northern counties to the Unionists with scarcely a murmur, and from then on never formulated a worthwhile policy of removing the border and uniting the country. On the contrary they opposed all forms of republicanism, including the removal of the oath of allegiance to the British throne, with an almost pathological fury and hatred. The present Fine Gael party has continued these policies since, with one honourable exception when John A. Costello was Taoiseach. They seem to want some kind of a solution to the Northern problems, if for nothing else but their own peace of mind, but I cannot find any evidence that they want a united Ireland with a parliament in Dublin containing seventy Ulster members. The official policy of the party is far closer to the British point of view than to the concept of a united Ireland envisaged by Pádraig Pearse or Michael Collins. It is only fair to add that a worthwhile number of Fine Gael grass roots would not go along with that policy.

Fianna Fáil as a political party, ironically enough, adopted to itself the policy of Michael Collins to dismantle the Anglo-Irish Treaty of 1921 bit by bit until a republic had been achieved. Collins had made a top-priority of Partition but Eamon de Valera, who founded and led Fianna Fáil, while making it an integral part of his policy did not give it the same transcendant importance. The craftiness of the politician was never far below the surface of De Valera's republicanism and it was the dextrous combination of these two that brought him such success. When Mr de Valera came to power in 1932 he devoted the next five or six years of his political life to removing the oath of allegiance to the king, demoting and later abolishing the office of governor-general, withholding the land annuities, re-occupying the British-held ports in Ireland and giving the country a completely new constitution which in Articles 3 and 4 laid claim to the whole island of Ireland. This, of course, included the North.

This was a tremendous achievement in a few short years. He had lifted the country out of the despondency into which it had fallen and he made men and women feel proud to be Irish once again. Sadly the Fine Gael party opposed him on every one of these issues, and indeed actively co-operated with the British to bring about his defeat.

Mr de Valera's anti-Partition speeches gave freshening hope to the sorely oppressed Nationalists in the Six Counties. They believed that at last someone in the South cared about them sufficiently to take some action. But these hopes proved illusory. For the rest of his political life Mr de Valera, apart from making speeches, did virtually nothing to come to grips with the partitioning of his country or to alleviate in any way the sufferings of the Nationalist population to whom he had given so much hope. During the short periods in the late 'forties and early 'fifties when he was out of office his oratory once more directed itself towards Partition:

> They tell you that what they called Ulster must not be coerced. Answer them that it is being coerced, that the majority of the people of four of the cut-off counties and the great minority in the rest are being held in territory garrisoned by British arms against their own wishes to unite with the rest of Ireland.

Again:

> We in Ireland will definitely regard as a hostile act any declaration that we have to convert a minority in the Six Counties — a minority so arranged that it has a perpetual majority in government.

And again:

> No Irish leader will ever be able to get the Irish people to co-operate with Great Britain while Partition remains.

This kind of talk gave great heart to the Nationalist population in the Six Counties. But unfortunately their expectations came to naught. When De Valera got back into power again he dropped the whole Partition issue like a hot potato. The student of *realpolitik* would say that he made these speeches to win back the republican vote he had lost to a new party, Clann na Poblachta and to regain office once more.

His successor, Seán Lemass, apart from going to Stormont to have afternoon tea with Lord O'Neill, showed himself equally disinclined to take any real practical steps to come to grips with the problem. It should in fairness to

Lemass be said that he is reputed to have asked both De Gaulle and Adenauer to block Britain's entry into the EEC until she left Northern Ireland, but how far that line was pursued is as yet unknown.

In 1969 when the present troubles burst upon the North and when the RUC and Unionist gangs were on a rampage of murder, burnings and evictions, deputation after deputation came down from the North to the Fianna Fáil government, then headed by Jack Lynch, and begged almost on their knees for some help. Their requests were refused. Later on when gas was being used against them they pleaded with Dublin to at least give them gas-masks. This appeal also went unheeded. Kevin Boland, one of the men of honour and integrity in this whole business, and who later resigned his post as cabinet minister, had the following to say of this shameful episode:

> I watched the performance particularly at government level with growing revulsion and with growing disillusionment. Here was the Republican Party (Fianna Fáil) in time of national crisis and national opportunity. . . From May 1970 to November 1970 I had the opportunity to survey the parliamentary party and I was sickened by what I saw — an almost complete lack of principle — one idea only — to avoid a general election, to avoid the possibility of losing one's seat!

Young men of idealism both North and South, no longer saw in Fianna Fáil the party of their ideals. Apart altogether from the North they had seen its steady decline. They had seen such ideals as love of country and love of language humiliated and suppressed. They now saw Fianna Fáil as just one more West British grouping who would not lift a finger to help the North.

In a radio interview in June 1982 Mr Neil Blaney MEP, too, recalled those days: 'The Fianna Fáil government should,' he said, 'have sent the Irish army across the border and forced a showdown with Stormont and with the British government. What stopped Jack Lynch was lack of decisiveness and lack of deep-seated convictions based on knowledge of the situation allied to a fear of the consequ-

49

ences. The army should have moved in at the time,' continued Mr Blaney. 'Generations have sought it and we funked it, really on 1 August 1969. The prime minister of Britain delayed sending in the British troops for forty-eight hours. It was a deliberate ploy because he foresaw the mess and if the Irish army went in he would have avoided all that.'

But perhaps the bitterest pill the Nationalists had to swallow was the realisation that Eamon de Valera co-operated fully with the Fianna Fáil government in abandoning them to their fate and in providing the help of the Irish army, the Irish police force and the Irish courts to assist the British in maintaining the statelet. He was President of Ireland at the time. All he had to do was to lift the telephone and threaten to resign. If he did so the government would certainly have jumped in line. In his book *The Rise and Decline of Fianna Fáil* Kevin Boland has this to say:

> . . . De Valera himself, who in less relevant times had left the Republican case on record all around the world, continued on as President of the Twenty-six County state and as commander-in-chief of the army, which was acting in full support of the British effort to impose military solutions.

Future biographers of De Valera will certainly have problems in trying to reconcile his speeches with his actions on the whole Northern question. In view of this attitude of De Valera it is hard to blame young Nationalists if they see him as both fraudulent and phoney — certainly a harsh point of view on such an outstanding figure but an understandable one.

Neither political party seems greatly disposed towards taking any real steps, apart from making speeches, to bring about a united Ireland. Not only that, but they are still spending vast sums of the Irish taxpayers' money to help the British army, the SAS and the RUC along the border. Early in 1982 we had a change of government, from a Fine Gael-dominated coalition to a Fianna Fáil administration. An editorial in the London *Times* aptly summed up their attitudes:

> In the more important matter of policing political terrorism, if past form is a guide, a change of government will not of itself make any difference.

This was a clear recognition by the British that no matter what party came to power in the South they could expect the full co-operation of that party in helping the RUC and the army. Surely this co-operation can only mean that both parties want the Northern Ireland statelet to remain?

I have always been curious as to why Fianna Fáil with its long republican tradition has been so indifferent in a practical sense to the unification of the country. So I put the question to a prominent Fianna Fáil politician, a man well versed in *realpolitik*. His answer was most revealing:

'Supposing we had a thirty-two county republic,' he said. 'What do you think Dáil Éireann would be like? With the North in we would have an extra seventy seats of which at least fifty could be held by Unionists. Can you not imagine what chaos this would cause? Fianna Fáil would never again be able to get an overall majority. It would be the end of party dominance, and I may tell you the end of a lot of jobs and Mercedes for the boys. The Unionists would permanently hold the balance of power; indeed we might very easily have a Unionist Taoiseach in a coalition. No matter how much we care about the plight of the Nationalists in the North, we do not care all that much. No. What we want in the North is some kind of peace, so that we won't be troubled by them — they're a bloody nuisance. Oh no, a united Ireland would be a disaster for us. But,' he added with a grin, 'if the Unionists had any damn sense that's what they'd be looking for.'

The comments of this man were not meant to be cynical or sarcastic. They were an open expression of the hard, raw, unpalatable facts upon which modern Irish politics are built — the very essence of *realpolitik*.

I do not think, therefore, it is widely off the mark to suggest that there is little evidence to show that either of the parties, despite their speeches, have any serious commitment to a united Ireland. The *Sunday Times* put it succinctly: 'They did not want the North but they did not want to admit that they did not want it.'

An even more telling comment was made in a BBC interview by Mr Humphrey Atkins, former Secretary of State for Northern Ireland. He said: 'It is my belief that if we were to say to the government of the Republic: all right, we will leave Northern Ireland, you can have it, they would turn and run. They don't want it.'

And what is of special interest is that *neither of the Irish political parties have contradicted any of these statements.*

The Tricolour has been taken down and, it seems, the Jolly Roger hoisted in its stead. But the tragedy of all this is that it has cost so much misery and so many human lives, dotted the countryside with so many graves, and it has thrown half-a-million Nationalists to the wolves.

Number Five: The British army is in Ireland as a peace-keeping force.

Outside Northern Ireland the British like to portray the role of the army as that of a kind of fairy godmother protecting the innocent, seeing them safely to their homes at night, if not exactly tucking them into bed. One young British officer in a military bar said to me: 'We are in Northern Ireland to try to preserve some form of civilised living.' I think he was hurt when I told him with some derision that very few people in Northern Ireland would accept that view, and indeed most would laugh at its naïvety.

The present state of the British army, not only in Northern Ireland but everywhere else is believed to be causing serious concern at the War Office itself. Drunkenness among all ranks is on the increase. More British soldiers have been killed in drunken driving accidents in Western Germany than by the IRA in Northern Ireland. The cult of violence is not only confined to civilians but is being demonstrated on the soldiers themselves by their comrades. An ex-British officer writing in the *New Statesman* on this sad state of affairs says:

> The psychopathic personality is common in the army, for it is the promise of 'aggro' which attracts many men into

uniform. Mass TV coverage of the army's role in the Ulster tragedy made recruitment rise dramatically and I have heard soldiers who have served in Northern Ireland boast that they put broken razor blades or nails into rubber bullets to make sure they hurt someone. One weapons' instructor lovingly described to me how he surprised an IRA sniper and cut him in half with close range machine-gun fire.

Unfortunately the record of these men who have been sent in to keep the peace in the North is nothing to be proud of. Their treatment of the Nationalist population is only marginally better than the treatment of the inhabitants of occupied countries by the Gestapo; arrogant, oppressive and brutal. Indeed one can frequently see such items of graffiti on Belfast walls as *Nazi Brits Go Home.* They do not worry too much about who they shoot so long as it can be done in a publicly credible situation. Since the troubles began they have shot down more than two hundred un-armed men, women and children. They have maimed more than one thousand, used plastic bullets which they are forbidden to use in England but allowed to use against the Irish. One sergeant when asked by his superior officer if he would have any problems in shooting Catholics or Protest-ants answered, 'No sir, just so long as provided they're Irish.' In their house to house searches they have beaten up women, some pregnant, kicked little children, smashed furniture and family pictures, dragged young men and girls by the hair out into the street. In 1973 an army lieutenant was quoted in the *Manchester Guardian* as saying:

> You know when we were in Ballymurphy. . . we had these people really fed up with us, really terrified. I understand what refugees must feel like in Vietnam. . . after every shooting incident we would order fifteen hundred houses searched — fifteen hundred!

Another officer said:

> Ski-ing or mountain climbing has got nothing on a cordon and search when you get old Snodgrass out of bed at four in the morning and you go through his house like a dose of salts.

In an interview with the *Guardian* newspaper, a young paratrooper said:

> Although you moan about Ireland at least you're going to have a chance to shoot some bastard through the head. . .
> You're there to kill people and to see guys killed. . .

It is not hard to imagine the publicity these statements would get in the Irish media and the hysterical condemnation they would cause had they been made by the IRA!

Near the Kent seaside resort of Hythe the British have built a mock Irish town with Irish names over the shops and Irish graffiti such as 'Brits Out' decorating the walls. British army terrorist units are trained here to shoot at moving targets in windows and doorways as well as in rip-searching a house from top to bottom. A second mock Irish town has now been built at the Sennelage Ranges in West Germany. I wonder what kind of media outcry one could expect if the Irish government built a mock British town in the Curragh?

In the Ardoyne area Unionist gangs burned down Nationalist homes while the army stood with their backs to the arsonists and aimed their guns at the Nationalists. In 1974 during the Unionist strike the British army refused to take action against the Unionist intimidators. The soldiers, and indeed the RUC, told journalists that they had orders not to do so. If one ignores the official spokesmen and speaks to the rank and file most of them will tell you the hard truth. They will tell you that in the special training courses they undergo prior to taking up duty in Northern Ireland it is made quite clear to them that the enemy is the Nationalist population.

It would be pleasant to say that these incidents were the exceptions but unfortunately this is normal behaviour. Their conduct has been fully documented in responsible newspapers and publications. In 1972 the New York based *International League for the Rights of Man* reported:

> Evidence exists that the British army engages in widespread assaults on both a random and selective basis. . . those particularly affected are ex-internees. These are subjected to being continually arrested and frequently beaten.

A similar statement came from the London based *National Council for Civil Liberties*. Anyone caring to check this out should spend a few days strolling around the Nationalist areas in Belfast. Here the whole thing can be seen on the ground: Saracens firing shots into Nationalist areas; houses searched where furniture is broken and smashed 'To teach these fucking Irish a lesson'; spot checks where people, including pregnant women, are put up against a street wall, searched and beaten with rifle butts. There is hardly anyone living in a Nationalist area that has not experienced this brutal harassment. But one can travel freely through the Unionist areas without seeing a British soldier. Regrettably the British army have a long string of killings to their credit, and the few who ever appear in court are usually found not guilty. I have no later statistics, but up to 1980 the admitted figure of killings of *innocent* people by the security forces is 116. This figure *does not* include killings of Nationalists or other paramilitaries — just ordinary, innocent men, women and children. In the beginning the Nationalists treated the British army with courtesy and often gave them cups of tea in the street. But they learned their bitter lesson and this has long since ceased. Indeed Northern justice must have reached its most outlandish point when a young Nationalist was sentenced to *six months imprisonment* for writing NO TEA FOR DAD'S ARMY on the gable end of his house.

As well as these units of the regular army worse still was in store for the Nationalist population in the Special Air Services, or more generally known as the SAS. Whether one likes it or not these are in effect legalised terrorists. For the most part these specially trained men wear civilian clothes, travel in plain cars, carry knives, daggers, sub-machine-guns and the outlawed pump-action shotguns. They are also issued with a special glove, steel-lined and mailed so that it can tear a man's face to pieces. One of its special functions according to *British Army Land Operations Manual* is to set up special 'assassination parties'. The type of individual which can be found in this force may be judged from the methods used when they stormed the

Iranian embassy in London. Having felled one man with the butt of a rifle they then shot him twenty-five times. They put twelve bullets into another man and twenty bullets into yet another. Commenting on this operation Margaret Thatcher said it made her 'proud to be British'.

In the North they operate mostly along the border and especially in south Armagh. Their object is (1) to kill on sight and without trial suspected IRA leaders, and (2) to terrorise the Nationalist population by torture, blackmail and at times even murder. In the month of June 1972 thirty young civilians were shot from passing cars by the SAS. So bad were their activities that the Civil Rights Association had to publish a booklet called *What to Do if the SAS shoot at You*. One of the more chilling parts reads:

> Provided you are alive when the shooting stops, pretend to be dead until the squad moves away, otherwise they might try to finish the job. If there is any army post nearby do not worry. It will not be manned or if it is the occupants will be busy writing a press statement to say that no military personnel were involved in the shooting.

One of the most frightening books ever written on Northern Ireland has been written by two priests, Fathers Denis Faul and Raymond Murray entitled *SAS Terrorism — The Assassin's Glove*. This is a history of the atrocities committed by this unit in Northern Ireland backed up by signed, witnessed statements, photographs and maps. Reading it makes one almost lose faith in human nature.

One member of the SAS told journalists in Dublin that his job was to cause explosions and bombings in Northern Ireland so that the IRA would be blamed. Seemingly he spoke out of turn. Shortly afterwards he was shot dead by his erstwhile colleagues.

One cannot also rule out the possibility that there is a certain amount of experimentation being carried out by the British army in Northern Ireland. This is the first campaign in a developed society which is a part of what is supposed to be a democracy. New techniques, new methods and new weapons are being tried out. All these, or some of the more successful may be used later in riot-control in Britain itself. In this sense the military lessons to be learned in Northern Ireland might well be seen to be worth the cost in lives and money. The callousness of such a policy is by no means outside the orbit of the British ruling classes.

I think I could not be accused of exaggerating if I suggest that there is much more than a doubt hanging over the activities of the British army in Northern Ireland. And if the forces of law and order do not administer justice and are themselves guilty of criminal acts then one can begin to understand how young men like Bobby Sands are forced to resort to violence.

I have felt it necessary to deal at some length with these statements because both in the South and abroad they have been accepted by many without question. The contrary is, of course, true of the North. Very few people up there believe them. In the hangman's house one naturally understands quite a lot about ropes.

The upshot of all this is that we should not accept without question everything the media tells us about Northern Ireland, nor should we place too much credence in the orations of cabinet ministers or politicians. And I would like to end this chapter with a special word to politicians and semi-politicians in the South: if you must make a speech condemning someone in Northern Ireland first of all check your facts fully from all sides. Secondly, the most Christian thing to do in this highly inflammable situation is to try to understand the forces, rational or irrational, that propelled these people into acts which seem to merit your condemnation. Ask yourself honestly what you would do if you were put into the defenceless situation in which they find themselves. Remember you may sometimes have to hide the truth from others – but you should never hide it from yourself. In that way you may save yourself many a foolish and unhelpful speech, and perhaps save a few lives as well.

3

The Beginning

The very moment the name of Ireland is mentioned the
English bid adieu to common feeling, common prudence
and common sense and act with the barbarity of tyrants and
the fatuity of idiots.

SYDNEY SMITH

I have never said and I am not going to say now that force is
not a legitimate weapon for a nation to use in striving to win
its freedom. I know that in history it is seldom that foreign
tyrants have ever yielded to any other. I have believed and
still believe that if a nation held in subjection by a foreign
power were to exclude altogether the idea of using physical
force to free itself, it would in effect be handing itself over
as a bound slave without hope of redemption. It is a long
wait they destine themselves to who rely on their tyrants
suffering a change of heart.

EAMON DE VALERA

While England explains the futility of force by others, it is
the only argument she listens to.

MICHAEL COLLINS

Bobby Sands was born in Newtownabbey in March 1954.
By and large Newtownabbey could be called a Unionist
area but because the family name did not sound particularly Gaelic they seemingly escaped the notice of the
Unionist paramilitaries. This, however, was not to last for
long. His father, John and his mother, Rosaleen kept a low
profile and lived a quiet unobtrusive life. Bobby, the eldest
was followed by three other children, Marcella in April
1955, Bernadette in November 1958 and John in June 1962.

Bobby grew up like any normal child, immersed in his
own little world where wickedness was unknown, living
airily from day to day and bit by bit entering into the

possession of his own self. Around his home he played with his young companions, full of innocence and trust with no real knowledge of the hard future that was to strangle his carefree golden world.

When Bobby was six years old the Unionists found out that the family was both Catholic and Nationalist and then began a subtle form of intimidation and harassment that was such a feature of life for the minority in Northern Ireland. The effect of this campaign against a helpless, inoffensive family took a heavy toll on the health of Mrs Sands and peace of mind of the family, so they decided to leave the area altogether. They vacated their home and lived with various relatives until finally after six months searching they managed to get another house in Doonbeg Drive in the Rathcoole district in 1961.

This was Bobby's first introduction to violence and hatred, and the beautiful world of love and understanding that was his had now received a menacing blow. His childlike confidence in the goodness of human beings was shattered, and it must have been about this time that the harsh reality that he was born a Nationalist began to dawn on his youthful mind. Years later when the situation had worsened he wrote:

> The whole world exploded and my own little world crumbled around me. The TV did not have to tell the story now for it was on my own doorstep. Belfast was in flames but it was our districts, our humble homes, which were burned. The Specials came at the head of the RUC and Orange hordes, right into the heart of our streets, burning, shooting, looting and murdering.

Many thousands of other young Nationalist children awakened to the same nightmare of terror, the same ending to their dreams of a normal childhood. In periodic raids gangs of Unionists, helped by the notorious B Special Police, drove them from their homes, burned and smashed their meagre furniture, beat and sometimes killed their parents, relatives and friends. Today one can walk through those little streets of ruined, burnt-out dwellings, empty and deserted like gaping skulls. It is a salutary exercise.

The tragedy is that so few do. The ruling classes who decide the fate of the province, the Irish politicians of the South who speak from the safety of comfortable homes, might very well learn a great deal if they visited these devastated areas more often, and reflected on the responsibilities resting upon them to see that this is brought to an end.

It is all so hard to grasp in the enlightened twentieth-century, but the evidence is there, full and loud and clear. Later on Bobby was to write:

> Although I never really understood. . . who the Specials were, I grew to regard them as symbols of evil. . . I was only a working-class boy from a Nationalist ghetto but it is repression that creates the revolutionary spirit of freedom.

The profound truth of that last sentence seems to have passed the British and Irish politicians by.

Bobby went to the Stella Maris primary school where he proved himself a student of much more than ordinary intelligence. Later on he went to secondary school at Rathcoole, as did also his young friend Mary Doyle who was to become one of the leaders of the protests in Armagh women's prison.

Yet despite the shadow of fear hovering over him his school days were ones of modest happiness. He became a budding ornithologist and nature lover and went on picnics to nearby Carnmoney Hill with his sisters and friends. In those long summer days of youth all nature began to open up to him, the soft sunshine falling on the earth, the clear blue sky, the long green grass, the trees and hedges alive with the hue of flowers, the humming of bees and the music of birds. It was here he saw his first lark, which was to become for him a life-long symbol of freedom. These days were to be the inspiration for many of his poems:

> There came a splendid golden sun,
> Across the darkened skies,
> It woke the bondsman from his dream,
> As it fell upon his eyes.
> It lit the ways of freedom's path,
> Sent forth the singing lark,
> And bore a weeping blossom on
> The flowers in the dark.

In these magnificent surroundings he was able to forget for a while the fear and terror that was slowly becoming part of his young life. Years later, in the stench of his prison cell in the Long Kesh concentration camp, he was to remember those days:

> My mind conjures up images of smiling girls and laughing children, sunny days and summer evenings. God, I long to be free with my family. I long to be far away from the evils that confront me each day. My body is dying before it's time. . . How I long for a walk through the countryside, to touch the lush green grass where there are open spaces, to hear the birds sing and to breathe the fresh, clean air, to live again. I'm not living now. I'm being tortured to death in this vile tomb, where they have held me naked for so long and in so much pain.

Like the temptations of the great saints, here one detects a hint of the temptation to give up.

When Bobby left secondary school he went to the local technical school and was later apprenticed to a coach-building firm in the Rathcoole industrial estate. Rathcoole was a mixed area with a large Unionist majority and when it was found out that the Sands were a Nationalist and Catholic family the cruel intimidation started again. But this time there was a new approach. There was living in this area a certain Unionist lady who knew where all the Nationalist houses were. If a young Unionist couple decided to get married they came to this woman and she drove them around the estate pointing out Nationalist houses to them. When they had chosen the house they wanted she passed along the word to the gangs and the intimidation started.

Bernadette Sands, Bobby's sister, describes what happened to them:

> I even saw them myself. Her standing outside our door and showing a young couple our house. Then about a week later we were put out. A rubbish bin was put through the living room window, stones were thrown and there was a couple of shots fired. My mother went down to the Housing Executive the next morning and told them that we'd have to get out there and then. They told her to head up to the Twinbrook office. The girl there told her to take whatever

61

house she could find free, put her curtains up, put some furniture in, and go back and tell the Executive the number. So that is how we got our house. We were promised that a lorry would come to take the furniture away from the house in Rathcoole and we had the cooker, the fridge and everything put into the front hall ready for a quick move, but the lorry did not turn up for days. Bobby was minding the house and this neighbour came over and said to him: 'Get your furniture out. I've a young couple to go into that house'.

The estate to which the Sands family moved, Twinbrook, was composed in the main of families who had been evicted or burned out by Unionist gangs. Some had no furniture left, others had to make do with houses only half-completed. There were numerous problems with milk for young children, fuel and food, but by working together and helping each other the thousands who had been driven into this ghetto managed to survive.

It is hard for people living in their secure comfortable homes outside Northern Ireland to realise the fear and terror that grips a Nationalist family intimidated out of two homes and wondering how long they will survive in the third. This is especially hard when they know that the forces of law and order are on the side of the intimidators.

But even worse was yet to come. Bobby was ordered at gun-point to give up his job. Before that he was waylaid on his way home one evening by a Unionist gang who stabbed him several times with knives and left him badly wounded. He barely made his way home, half-crawling, half-staggering.

A series of terrible questions suggest themselves here. Did these doomed and hapless people get any help from the British government? Did they get any help from the ecclesiastics? Did the Southern government do anything to help them? Did we, the people of the South, lift a finger to come to their aid? In all cases the answer is 'No'. And when in despair these unfortunate people took the law into their own hands, a share of the blame for what followed must rest on all our shoulders. We all helped to build that first tier of violence, which in turn produced the second tier and in its turn produced the third. Like the priest on the road to Jericho we left the victim to suffer and die.

It has been often said that while we in the South never lacked intelligence or imagination, we very frequently lacked character. From time to time I have spoken to many of the politicians in the South who have condemned the Nationalists in the North and put the following question to them: 'Supposing *you* were in Bobby Sands' shoes,' I asked, 'kicked out of your home twice, threatened, beaten-up, stabbed and intimidated out of your job and livelihood, what exactly would *you* do?' In almost all cases they just stared at me as if I had slapped them in the face and moved away. I could hardly blame them. When the paramilitaries put the same questions to me I funked it too. But at least I did not make any condemnatory speeches.

This is an incisive, penetrating question which each one of us should put to ourselves. By trying in the silence of our own souls to answer this question honestly and truthfully we will have gone a long way towards understanding the problem of Northern Ireland. This is a *realpolitik* question.

One of the milder criticisms that has been levelled at Northern Nationalists is that they tend to regard 1969 as the year in which the fight for Irish freedom began. This is probably an understandable point of view because it was in the years 1969-70 that these beleagured people really put in the boot and cried: 'Stop! We've had enough!' It was also at this time that graffiti began to appear on the walls of Belfast with the words *Never Again*. For fifty years, without success they had tried peaceful, non-violent means of getting the very basic civil rights as citizens. Now their mood changed. Never again would they turn the other cheek to the Unionists. They would stand their ground and hit back with bullets if necessary. This is how violence is born. This is the second tier described by Archbishop Camera. But to begin they would try less violent means.

While this change of mood was the logical outcome of their bitter frustration they were, unlike earlier generations, inspired and encouraged to a very considerable degree by the success of other civil rights movements throughout the world, particularly in the United States. They saw that when ordinary, under-privileged people took to the streets in protest marches the ruling classes could not ignore them. And so the Northern Ireland Civil Rights Association (NICRA) became the spearhead of their action.

The first major protest march took place in October 1968 in Derry city. The Nationalist population of Derry had a majority over the Unionist population, but on account of the gerrymandering the Unionists controlled the city council. About two thousand marchers headed by Labour MP Gerry Fitt started from Waterside but they had scarcely gone a few hundred yards when they were set upon and savagely batoned by a huge force of police. The marchers had nothing to fight back with and so these merciless attacks and beatings continued until the march was broken up.

Perhaps the most important of these marches was one modelled on the famous march from Selma to Montgomery in Alabama in 1966 which threw the spotlight on the racial mobsters of the south and forced the American government to make important and far-reaching legal reforms. The marchers started off in Belfast to walk to Derry about seventy miles away, and in time a matter of a few days. They had hopes that the march, like its American counterpart, might produce similar results, especially as the new Unionist premier, Captain Terence O'Neill, had given faint signs that he was a man of liberal outlook who would have some sympathy for their plight. Only about eighty marchers, mostly students, started out from Belfast City Hall on New Year's Day 1969. The march was not banned because the government thought it would fizzle out but instead it gained in strength all along the route and when it finally reached Derry it had swollen to hundreds.

In almost every village through which they passed they were attacked and stoned by Unionist mobs while the police not only stood by and watched, but in some cases laughed and joked with the attackers.

On 4 January when they were on the last leg of their journey and a short distance outside the village of Claudy they were stopped by some police who seemed unusually friendly and who gave them specific directions as to how to proceed. After a few minutes they carried on somewhat bewildered at the amiable attitude of the men in uniform. They were soon to find out why. They had been manoeuvred into a deadly trap. A short distance ahead at Burntollet Bridge hundreds of Unionists had lain in ambush and they now attacked the marchers with rocks, stones and broken bottles, which they had been collecting for days before. They had taken up carefully prepared positions on a height overlooking the route and when they had exhausted their supply of missiles they rushed headlong on the confused marchers and attacked them with iron bars and clubs. These unfortunate people, tired and hungry after the long trek, took a terrible beating before they finally broke through to continue their march. All the while this was happening the police looked on and took no corrective action whatever against the attackers. It was later learned that a large number of the attackers were actually members of the auxiliary police in civilian clothing.

This incident was to have a profound effect on Bobby Sands:

> My sympathy and feelings really became aroused after watching the scenes at Burntollet (on TV). That imprinted itself on my mind like a scar, and for the first time I took a real interest in what was going on. I became angry.

That historic march to Derry seems to have been a turning point in the affairs of Northern Ireland. Up to this point the Unionists had everything very much their own way. When they cracked the whip the frightened minority cowed under and hid in terror. They even paraded through Nationalist areas to show they were the lords. But this dejected attitude of servility had at last come to an end. A young, new, intelligent minority of ever-increasing numbers refused to turn the other cheek no matter how savagely they were treated and they planned and carried out more and more marches.

The reaction of the Unionists and the police to the new attitude can only be described as psychopathic in the extreme. After a provocative march by the Apprentice Boys in August 1969 in Derry, they invaded the Nationalist areas and attacked the population in a series of riots, raids, onslaughts, rampages and harassments. Police entered the home of Sam Deveney and beat him in front of his screaming family to such an extent that he died weeks later from his wounds. Later they beat another, Francis McCloskey, to death and in Belfast they again beat yet another, Patrick Corry, to death in front of relatives and friends who had to watch these outrages and console these poor men in their last agony. Again in Belfast the police went beserk and fired indiscriminately into Nationalist areas killing Patrick Rooney and Herbert McCabe and wounding several others. Unionist gangs, helped by the auxiliary police, set fire to whole streets in minority areas. On the night of 14/15 August 1969 alone five Nationalists were killed, hundreds injured and one hundred and fifty families burned out of their homes. The story was the same across all of Northern Ireland and at last the British government realised that they had more than a riot on their hands and so sent in the British army to try to restore order and contain the situation.

Initially the Nationalist population rejoiced and hoped that the army would protect them but unfortunately this hope proved unfounded. It turned out that the British army were merely a substitute for the B Specials.

When Bobby was a child the British army were his TV heroes:

> The British army always fought for the 'right side' and the police were always the 'good guys'.

He was to wake up later to the hard reality:

> As the unfamiliar sound of gunfire was still echoing, there soon appeared alien figures, voices and faces, in the form of armed British soldiers on our streets. But no longer did I think of them as my childhood 'good guys', for their presence alone caused food for thought. Before I could work out the solution it was answered for me in the form

of early morning raids. From now on my heart pounded at the heavy clatter of the soldiers' boots in the early morning stillness and I carefully peered from behind the drawn curtains to watch the neighbours' doors being kicked in, the fathers and sons being dragged out by the hair and being flung into the backs of sinister-looking armoured cars. This was followed by blatant murder: the shooting dead of our people on the streets in cold blood.

Now the Nationalist population, virtually unarmed, found itself faced not only by the police, but the British army as well. In this desperate situation they sought help from their friends in the South only to find that nothing was forthcoming. In the South the politicians might be said to have covered their heads in the sand, and the leader of the government refused all help to the Nationalists. This refusal almost broke their spirit. They felt totally and completely let-down and betrayed. With everything and everyone against them they saw nothing ahead but the road to extermination.

It was when they had reached this very gloomy point of despair that a new hope appeared, a new force came into being, a force which in effect said: 'Do not give up. We will protect you!' That force came to be known as the Provisional IRA, or for short, the Provos. The violence had now escalated from civil rights marches to virtual civil war. Here again one must honestly pose the terrible *realpolitik* question: Are the Northern Nationalists to be blamed for supporting the gun? What other option had they?

The Official IRA had been fighting spasmodically in the North since the foundation of the state without any real success. In the late 'fifties and early 'sixties largely, but not only, because they had been infiltrated by members of the British Communist Party who sought to use the Republican movement to set up a Marxist front for political and social agitation, they had neither the will nor the means to defend or help the beleagured Nationalists. The Northern Brigade, disgusted with this failure broke away and founded a non-Marxist political movement, Provisional Sinn Féin and a military wing, the Provisional IRA. It was to this new movement that the Nationalist population turned. Later

Official Sinn Féin became the Workers Party and it is said that the Official IRA disbanded leaving the field to the Provos.

Over the next few months and years hundreds of young men and women joined this new force because they saw in it the only means to defend their homes and families from the attacks of the Unionist gangs, the police and the British army. One of these was young Bobby Sands.

When he joined the IRA he could well look back for inspiration to Ireland's most revered statesman, Eamon de Valera, who told British ambassador Sir John Maffey that if he (De Valera) were a young man belonging to the Catholic minority in Northern Ireland *he would be a member of the IRA*. Fianna Fáil politicians today like to gloss over this admission by their venerated founder.

The new Sinn Féin–IRA organisation stated its aims clearly and publicly:

> To establish a Thirty-two County Republic. . . to restore the Irish language and culture to a position of strength. . . to promote a social order based on justice and Christian principles. . . demands for civil rights, better housing, division of large estates, restoration of fishing rights, setting up of credit unions and worker-owned co-operatives are all elements in the building of a movement of the people. . .

Their immediate objective, however, was more urgent:

> . . .At the moment the greatest need of all is for assisting our people in the Six Counties in their demands for civil rights. Not only that but we must ensure adequate defence and protection for them so that they are not left at the mercy of Crown forces or sectarian bigots. . .

This last sentence is of major importance. It is in effect a *declaration of war* against the British government and the government of Northern Ireland. What is also of major importance is that both governments *accepted* that a state of war existed. The Northern Ireland premier, Major Chichester-Clarke publicly declared: 'Northern Ireland is at war with the Irish Republican Army Provisionals.' Reginald Maudling, British Secretary of State, also publicly declared that the British government was 'now in a state of open war with the IRA.' Archbishop Camera's third tier of violence had arrived.

Neither of them said: 'These are criminals engaged in civil commotion'. What in fact they said was that there was a war on and they subsequently acknowledged this by granting IRA prisoners prisoner-of-war status. They later changed their minds, not about the existence of a state of war, but about the status of prisoners-of-war. This change was to have far-reaching consequences.

Most of the Nationalist population, particularly in the ghettos, saw in the IRA their saviours and protectors. These young men believed they were the inheritors of the oldest guerrilla force in the world who had waged a war against the British for more than sixty years. They did not see themselves as terrorists because their object, unlike the SAS, was not to strike terror into civilians, but to shield and defend half-a-million Irish people from destruction and perhaps death and in the process to get rid of the occupying British whom they saw as the predominant cause of all this suffering.

This is how the Provisional IRA began and I think it behoves us all to take a hard cold look at these circumstances and not be influenced by any propaganda from any quarter. We must also ask ourselves some *realpolitik* questions: Who are really responsible for the birth of the Provisional IRA? Do we, here in the South, share in that responsibility by our indifference and inactivity towards a people whom we constitutionally claim to be our own? Before we begin to throw stones perhaps we might examine the structure of the glasshouse!

The first real confrontation came in June 1970, not with the British army, but with Unionist paramilitaries who attacked St Matthew's Catholic Church located in a small Nationalist enclave near the Short Strand surrounded on all sides by Unionists. When the attack started the British army were asked by an MP to come in and give some protection to the church, but they refused. The IRA then moved in and the battle started at about eleven o'clock at night and lasted until five o'clock in the morning. The object of the attackers was to burn the church to the ground and then burn the houses in the Nationalist enclave and so render almost two thousand people homeless. But the whole operation failed. The church was saved, as well as the people's homes, and the Unionists were driven back with two of their members dead. Many more died of wounds over the next few weeks. The actual number of casualties is not known but local people tell of several graves being dug at night for Unionist burials.

This particular incident had far-reaching effects. It showed the Unionists that they could no longer do as they pleased with the minority and it showed the Nationalists that they now had at last the nucleus of an army capable of giving them protection.

Substantial funds, especially from the United States, were donated to this new force which enabled them to arm themselves slowly with some of the most modern weapons. In 1970 they smuggled large quantities of the Armalite AR 15 which when used with tungsten-tipped bullets can penetrate the British armoured cars. They also provided themselves with quantities of the M 3, a silent gun known as the 'spitting dummy'; the M 42 which came from Greece; the USA M 1 Carbine which they use for close combat street fighting; the RPG-7 Rocket launcher; the Remington Woodmaster — a pump action sniping rifle; and the highly effective M 60 machine-gun which can fire 600 rounds per minute. Twelve of these latter were stolen from a US army base in West Germany.

Many of their members went abroad for crash training courses in guerrilla warfare — where exactly has been kept secret. When these men came home they in turn ran secret training camps both in the Six Counties and in Southern Ireland. One of these camps is believed to have been located at the beautiful green bog-island of Derrynaflan in Tipperary. This, it is said, had to be quickly abandoned when the famous ninth-century chalice was discovered there.

One of the hard facts, which so few people in the South seem to believe is that the Nationalist population accepted the new IRA — they housed them, fed them, hid them and whether we like it or not *this support continues down to the present day.* When I asked one young married woman living in a Nationalist area if she really supported the IRA despite the condemnations by church and state, she answered without hesitation: 'Of course I do and so do all my neighbours. Who else have we to protect us? You people in the South haven't a clue what it is like to live up here. If we hadn't the Provos we'd be as good as dead. Will you or your loud-mouthed politicians come up to help us?' I had no answer to her question.

The war continued and spread across the whole of Northern Ireland. There was a sad litany of killings, bombings, burnings, torture, imprisonment and sectarian murders. Then in 1972 it became clear that the Stormont government was unable to govern. It was dissolved and direct rule from London was imposed on the whole province. This, after sixty years of struggle, the IRA saw as their greatest achievement. And this was to give them a tremendous boost, and in the eyes of many to justify military action, that is to justify violence!

As well as the growing military activity by the IRA the Northern Civil Rights movement kept up their peaceful protest marches. One of these was to make headlines across the world.

It happened in Derry on 30 January 1972. A peaceful march of unarmed civilians in protest against internment without trial was taking place through the streets of that city. The British knew there were no IRA in the vicinity that day so it was later assumed that they decided to teach these rebellious natives a lesson they would not forget. Without warning they opened fire on the unarmed marchers, killing thirteen and wounding dozens of others. Derry will never forget that day which came to be known all over the world as 'Bloody Sunday' but in Unionist circles it was christened 'Good Sunday'. The comment of one eyewitness is well worth recording:

Fulvio Grimaldi, Italian press photographer:

I have travelled in many countries. I have seen many civil wars and revolutions. I have never seen such organised, cold-blooded, disciplined murder. . . I saw a young fellow who had been wounded crouching against the wall shouting, 'Don't shoot, don't shoot.' A paratrooper approached him and shot him from about one yard. I saw a young boy of fifteen protecting his girl friend against the wall. : . a paratrooper approached and shot him in the stomach and the girl in the arm.

Numbers of English, French, Italian and American journalists witnessed this terrible massacre, which once again blighted the name and reputation of the British army all over the world. Saddest of all was the fact that an English Catholic bishop justified the killings on the grounds that soldiers have to obey orders. This piece of theology should be a great relief in the next world to the commandants of Dachau, Belsen, Auschwitz and other concentration camps.

After the fall of Stormont the effective ruler of the North was a secretary of state appointed by the British prime minister. He was assisted by a junior minister. These officials were British politicians with very limited knowledge of the real conditions in Northern Ireland and usually when they began to know something about the country they were transferred. For the most part they were politicians whose primary commitment was to England and to the furtherance of British policy. Neither were they unmindful of the further advancement of their own careers. The plight of Northern Ireland itself could hardly be described as one of their top priorities. One or two of these officials were biased, ignorant and unprincipled and not a few were just downright stupid, conceited and arrogant.

Again what stung the Nationalist population was that there seemed to be little difference between the approach of the Dublin government and the approach of the British government on the problem of Northern Ireland. Both governments introduced most repressive legislation, such as courts not bound by standard laws of evidence, almost unlimited powers of arrest and interrogation. The Dublin government, however, went a step further than the British

by introducing legislation which prevented, and still prevents Nationalist paramilitaries from being interviewed on
Irish radio and television. We, therefore, have the position
here that a member of the IRA or one of the Sinn Féin
political wing may not appear on Irish radio or television
but Unionist paramilitaries may appear as often as the
programme-makers wish. No elected representative of
Sinn Féin anywhere may appear on our screens. One outstanding example at the present moment is that of Owen
Carron, Republican MP for Fermanagh and South Tyrone,
who was elected with a personal vote almost three times
larger than any Southern Irish politician. He cannot be
interviewed on our radio or televison but some of the
greatest Unionist fomentors of violence can, as well as
members of the British army.

When Bobby Sands, an elected MP, was alive he would
not be allowed to appear on Irish radio or television, but
the men who smashed up his home, who stabbed him
almost to death, who drove him at gun point from his job,
who tortured him in prison — these men could and can
appear without hindrance on our screens. All this has been
regarded as another unqualified and brilliant success of
British propaganda. It is of course important to say here
that most of the RTE journalists and presenters are in no
way responsible for this state of affairs. They have honourably and consistently sought to have this servile legislation
revoked. Nevertheless the *realpolitik* of the situation is that
the Irish government having abandoned the Nationalists in
the North, seem to be using this form of censorship to keep
the public of the Twenty-six Counties in the dark about
what is really happening across the border. They seemingly
do not want it to be known that the vacuum created by their
defection from their early ideals has been filled by others.

Almost from the moment the troubles started the
Catholic Church took an ambivalent stand but on the
whole they leaned towards the *status quo*. The reason given
for this was that they were taking the side of law and order.
The Nationalists, however, would say that the Church did
not enquire too closely into the morality of the law or the

ethics of the order and that the real reason they were backing Britain was that they saw in this course a surer method of holding on to and improving their own authority and power. This belief by many of the Catholic population drove a wedge between them and their leaders, nudged them into the arms of the IRA, and produced the present day situation where the Church as a political influence has probably reached its lowest point. One of the most enlightened of the Northern Bishops, Most Reverend Dr Cathal Daly used a rather unfortunate phrase in a recent interview with the *New York Times*. He is reported to have said '. . . we are not fighting for independence here. We are trying to find a peaceful political solution.' This would not command acceptance amongst all the Nationalist people who would say that not only do they want peace and independence, but they want justice as well. Later on we will see how Bobby Sands, a Catholic in this new mould, rejected the Church's political role, while accepting fully its pastoral mission.

Another matter which had a rather upsetting effect on the influence of the Church was the alleged attitude of some of the English chaplains in the British Army. Not only did they use their priestly calling to act as intelligence agents but they openly sided with the killings committed by the army on the grounds that the soldiers must obey and on occasions gave them special blessings before they embarked on a shooting campaign against the Irish.

The newly-found determination and courage of the Nationalists, of course, produced an immediate Unionist reaction. For fifty years they had been the undisputed overlords and bosses. Now their dominance was seriously challenged so they too took to a more highly organised form of violence and terrorism through their paramilitaries. These Unionist paramilitaries were composed of various splinter groups. It is simpler to refer to them as Unionist paramilitaries since the final objective of all groups was the same, namely the maintenance of the privileged majority in power with absolute control over the minority. They decided that the best way to regain power

BOBBY SANDS AND THE TRAGEDY OF NORTHERN IRELAND

was to terrorise and murder Nationalists irrespective of whether such were involved politically or not. It is now known that in this campaign they were discreetly helped by the police who regularly, and of course illegally, passed on vital information from confidential police files.

Their reign of terror is a sad blot on the history of Northern Ireland. Sectarian killings, burning of Nationalist homes and the destroying of Nationalist business premises were their principal methods. One or two examples out of hundreds will give some idea of the savagery of their campaign. James McCartan was kidnapped and brought to a premises in Clermont Lane, Belfast. He was stripped naked, hung upside down by the heels and beaten with clubs. He was stabbed several times then dragged to a waste ground and shot dead in the head. Another, Patrick Benstead was also kidnapped, brought to the same place, burned on the feet and hands with a red hot poker, then with the same poker his back was branded with a cross and his eyes gouged out. Another young man had his throat cut, his penis cut out, and stuffed down his throat wrapped in his rosary beads.

This litany of horror could go on and on, but instead of frightening the Nationalists it had the opposite effect. It strengthened their resolution and made them more and more determined to accept death rather than ever let these people back to power again.

So when Bobby Sands went into the Republican headquarters and joined the IRA, he had a fair assembly of forces lined up against him, the British government, the British army, the Irish government, the Unionist paramilitaries and both the Catholic and Protestant Churches:

I was born in a Protestant area of Belfast [he wrote]. I was keen on sports and won a lot of medals and ran for Protestant clubs. My family was intimidated out of our home and we moved to Twinbrook on the outskirts of Belfast. Soon after that I was intimidated from my workplace at gun-point. Shortly afterwards I joined the Republican movement. I had seen too many houses wrecked, fathers

75

and sons arrested, neighbours hurt, friends murdered, too much gas, shooting and blood.

He explains himself how he came to join the IRA:

> Easter 1972 came and the name on everyone's lips was 'the Provos', the people's army. I was now past my eighteenth year and I was fed up with rioting. No matter how much I tried, or how many stones I threw I could never beat them — the Brits always came back. At eighteen-and-a-half I joined the Provos and went out to meet and confront the might of an empire. . .

In opting for force he was not far removed from the philosophy of the Fianna Fáil founder, Eamon de Valera, who referred many times to Partition as a 'meditated crime' and who said: 'The Southern States of the American Union had a far better case for secession than our Northern Unionists have and President Lincoln faced four years of terrible civil war rather than permit it.' Again in the Senate in February 1939 he made it quite clear that he would use force if he could to end Partition. It is somewhat embarrassing for Fianna Fáil today to realise that both Eamon de Valera and Bobby Sands were agreed that the use of force to end Partition was justifiable. The only difference between them was that De Valera felt they were not strong enough to do so and would not succeed, while Bobby Sands felt that whether or not they could succeed they had no choice left. But on the principle of using violence as a means they were both at one.

It is an unpalatable fact that the circumstances which drove Bobby Sands to resort to force also drove hundreds if not thousands of other young people to take to the gun instead of trying to achieve their ends by peaceful means. But we must again be brutally honest and ask ourselves who created the circumstances in the first place and if these circumstances never existed would there be peace today? If our politicians feel they must condemn the IRA — and indeed that is their right in a free society — surely they should also condemn in even stronger terms those who either by commission or omission created the circumstances which brought about the IRA. They are the people who have built the first tier of violence, and they simply cannot cover their heads in the sand and escape responsibility. Could it be that many of those who are so strong in their condemnation of violence have a guilty conscience about their own part in the whole affair? To decide who are the guilty ones is at the very core of the Northern Ireland question — a question which requires *realpolitik* answers.

4

The Young Man

I decline to plead before this court because I don't recognise that this court has authority seeing it is the creature of a foreign power. . . I don't recognise the court.

EAMON DE VALERA
before a Belfast court, 1924

I believe, as do the vast majority, that the ideal way of ending Partition is by peaceful means. But no one has the right to assert that force is irrevocably out. No political party or group at any time is entitled to predetermine the right of the Irish people to decide what course of action on this question may be justified in given circumstances. The Fianna Fáil party has never taken a decision to rule out the use of force if the circumstances in the Six Counties so demand.

NEIL BLANEY, TD, MEP

We have watched Garret Fitzgerald's foolish and bungling attempts to appease the Unionists. I have yet to hear him speak of his concern for the Nationalist community who have had to endure so much hatred and discrimination. This is the section of the community in the North that look to the South for encouragement and help only to find that neither is forthcoming.

SILE DE VALERA, MEP

Bobby Sands had now lived through and personally experienced the cruel injustice of Unionist rule in his homeland. He saw the failure of peaceful means. He also knew that they could expect no help from the Southern government. He had seen how for so many long years their speeches had only served to raise false hopes in the suffering Nationalist population and to provide the Unionists with more ammunition to inflict still further injustices and oppressions.

Trapped like so many other young Irishmen in this hope-
less situation he believed that not only had he a duty to protect his fellow Nationalists but he also believed that British
rule had to be destroyed and that violence was now the last
resort. This was a decision which the first tier of violence,
the Violence of Injustice, forced upon him.

> The price of freedom is a terrible price [he later wrote].
> Many suffer that some day all Irishmen may know justice
> and peace. All of us must pay the price. . . All liberation
> struggles are bitter and more often than not they are all
> protracted bloody wars. . . Our own struggle bears no
> different mark.

Although he was strengthened by the awakened mood of
the people after such a long endurance he saw both the
danger and limitations of violence. In a passage of remarkable discernment he further wrote:

> It must be said that an armed people are by no means a sure
> guarantee to liberation. Our guns may kill our enemies but
> unless we direct them with the politics of a revolutionary
> people they will eventually kill ourselves. Guns don't win
> wars; guns and bombs may kill a man but they cannot lead a
> man. . . nor will they ever coerce an unyielding man to
> yield.

When Bobby Sands joined the IRA he knew it was not
going to be a life of ease and adventure. He was well aware
of the dangers and his decision was a fully informed one.
Perhaps the best description of the life he was embarking
upon was given in an interview by a Provisional IRA man
to Vincent Browne of *Magill:*

> You have to remember that life in the IRA is no bed of
> roses. There are no rich Provos. We have to suffer im-
> prisonment, torture, being constantly on the run, isolated
> from our families. . . There is also the factor of being con-
> stantly misrepresented and condemned by the supposed
> moral leaders of our society.

When Bobby Sands made his decision to join the IRA
and to resort to violence as a means of protecting and free-
ing his people he could look back on a long line of distinguished Irishmen who took the same course: Pearse, Con-

nolly and the other 1916 leaders; Eamon de Valera, Michael Collins, Seán Mac Eoin, Dan Breen, Tom Barry, Terence MacSwiney and hundreds of others including Garret Fitzgerald's father, Desmond Fitzgerald. These men, who are now held in the highest esteem were in their day called 'criminals', 'thugs', 'murderers', 'gangsters', by the same elements that today are using these same words to describe Bobby Sands *viz.* the British, the Church, the politicians, the media. But they persevered and won freedom for a part of their country. Yet the men who succeeded them in government, the well-heeled politicians seem strangely unmindful that what they have they owe to those who took up the gun when all branches of the Establishment of the day condemned them, including the Church who excommunicated them. This little matter is now conveniently overlooked.

When a young man like Bobby Sands joins a paramilitary group he is not, of course, ready for active service immediately. He has to go through fairly intensive courses in the use of weapons, mines, bombs, movement, field craft, intelligence and street-fighting. There are, as well, specialist courses particularly in electronics which has now become a vital element in the war. For example the British invented a special anti-ambush device attached to their vehicles which immediately indicated from where the ambushers' shots came. The IRA countered this by setting up decoys so that when the British jumped out from their lorries they were attacked from an entirely different direction. The British also devised an invisible ray beam by which spotters in helicopters could see all movement on the ground in the dark. These helicopters are used by the British south of the border with a blanket permission of the Dublin government. The IRA have found that these spotter rays are useless in heavy rain or high winds so they use this type of weather to mount their attacks. They also use American army infra-red binoculars with special night vision to spot the helicopters several miles away. According to the British army's leading explosive expert the IRA bombs are amongst the most perfect in the world and are daily getting more and more sophisticated and deadly. All this requires a very high degree of skilled training and is a far cry from the old days of guerrilla warfare where a cart was shoved across the road at a bend and an ambush laid. There are also anti-interrogation courses which tend to prepare a volunteer for the methods of torture used at interrogation centres such as Castlereagh, Gough and Strand Road, and which conditions them not to break under police cruelties.

Because of the nature of the paramilitaries these courses have to be spread out over a long period of time, but in the short term new members can be used for limited activities such as surveillance of police, military or suspected informers, protection duty, transporting active service members from one place to another.

Since I was given to understand that there was a security problem involved I could not ascertain who recruited Bobby, or any specific details about his training. However, as far as I could find out he did undergo a basic training in the use of small arms. He was then assigned to general auxiliary duties and it was the intention, since he was a highly intelligent individual, to put him on more advanced training in the winter of 1972. He was of course by now known to the police and army as an IRA member.

> My life now centred around sleepless nights and stand-bys [he wrote]. Dodging the Brits and calming the nerves to go out on operations. But the people stood by us. They not only opened the doors of their homes to lend us a hand but they opened their hearts to us. I learned that without the people we could not survive and I know that I owed them everything.

In all guerrilla warfare the strongest weapon the guerrillas have is the goodwill of the people. It was this weapon that won the Anglo-Irish War in 1918-1921 and it was the absence of the same weapon that lost the Civil War for the Republicans in 1922-1923. In Northern Ireland the IRA were able to make full use of this weapon insofar as the vast majority of Nationalist homes were open to them, particularly in the ghettos and the rural areas, and I can find no evidence to suggest that such is not the case at the present moment.

When I was researching this book I came across a curious incident which intrigued me and gave me an unusual insight into the value of opinion polls. Some outfit or other was conducting a public opinion poll in Belfast as to the attitude of the people to the IRA. In one small house in a Nationalist area the housewife was asked if she approved of the IRA and in strong, vehement language she expressed her disapproval of them and everything they stood for and almost threw the questioner out for daring to ask such a question. The enquirer duly noted this for his statistics. What she did not say of course was that at that very moment two IRA men on the run were asleep in a room upstairs. Her native cunning had told her that there was a danger any answer she made might ultimately find its way into the computer at police headquarters, so she stretched the truth somewhat and the media were able to give us another researched statistic!

Bobby Sands was now a marked man on the police files and he knew it would be only a matter of time before they picked him up. He did not, however, expect it so soon. One morning in autumn 1972 he was travelling by car with three friends and when they arrived in Lisburn the car was stopped by the police who addressed Bobby by his name. Seemingly they were expecting him which would point to the fact that they were acting on a tip-off. The others were released and he was brought to one of the RUC centres, politely known as 'interrogation centres'. There he was put through the type of interrogation, with torture, which was the normal procedure adopted by the police to obtain convictions against the Nationalists.

Torture of Nationalist suspects was the accepted norm and was carried out with the knowledge and approval of the British government. This was clearly shown later when that government was convicted at the Court of Human Rights in Strasbourg. Many of the officials responsible for the torture were subsequently promoted instead of being punished and later the Queen of England graciously con-

ferred honours on some of them. One can imagine the outcry in the media if the President of Ireland even received an
IRA bomber! But when the Queen bestowed her honours
most of the Irish media made obeisance in silence.

The methods of torture used in Northern Ireland by both
the British army and the police are based on techniques
successfully used by the Gestapo, the KGB and the South
African police, and perfected by the British in Cyprus, Aden
and Kenya. In the terrible Hola prison in Kenya prisoners
who were not even charged were made work scraping dry
earth with their bare hands in temperatures of 120F while
their British army guards lashed and beat them. The excuse
given by the then English Secretary of State for Defence was:
'Experience has shown, time after time, that unless hard-core
detainees can be got to start working their rehabilitation is impossible!' This prompted Mr Sidney Silverman MP to intervene and ask, 'Who told the Right Hon. Member that? Stalin?'

The methods used in Northern Ireland are mainly:

1. Making a man stand in what is known as the 'search'position, i.e. single finger only of each hand touching the wall,
legs apart and far back resting on the toes with knees bent,
for long periods. This was a speciality of the Nazis and
Russians and was known as the 'Stoika'.
2. Kicking the legs from under a man in the search position
so that he falls and batters his head on the ground.
3. Heavy beatings with batons on the kidneys and testicles
in the search position.
4. Kicking the testicles while in the search position. For
some reason this is quite popular with the police.
5. Stretching a man over benches with two powerful
electric fires under him thus burning his privates and then
kicking him from underneath in the stomach.
6. Banging a man's head against a wall, beating it with a
rubber baton for long periods.
7. Squeezing the testicles with a large pincers. The police
say that the excruciating pain of this will make a man sign
almost anything.
8. The use of electric instruments, such as a cattle prod.

9. Inserting iron instruments up the anus and bursting it.
10. Finger searching the anus and then sticking the un-
washed finger in the prisoner's mouth.
11. Tying the prisoner flat on the ground and several police
urinating on him.
12. The pyschological torture includes Russian roulette
with a revolver, beating men in the darkness, threats
against a prisoner's parents, spouse and children and the
use of amphetamine drugs.

These methods of torture shock all right-thinking people
but evidently not the British government or the police.
According to the magazine *Police Beat* in July 1979 a
representative of the Northern Police Federation said:

> The concentrated attack on the interrogation procedures
> which culminated in the Bennett Report will do nothing but
> hamper the defeat of terrorism. If the hands of the police
> are tied still further then undoubtedly more gunmen and
> bombers will go free. . .

Hundreds of statements from prisoners have been published confirming this torture and there has scarcely been a
book written on Northern Ireland which has not dealt with
it in one way or another. Gerry Fitt MP said in the House of
Commons: 'When the true story emerges of what has been
happening in the interrogation centres the people of the
United Kingdom will receive it with shocked horror and
resentment.'

We do not know in detail how many of these techniques
were used on Bobby Sands after his first arrest as he was
always reticent in telling anyone about his sufferings in case
these distressful details came to the ears of his parents and
caused them undue anguish and pain. Instead of recounting
his sufferings to others he usually wrote them down and we
have detailed written accounts of his treatment. He does
not seem to have written anything later on about this first
interrogation.

When he was charged in autumn 1972, like de Valera,
he refused to recognise this Belfast court, but reserved the
right to cross-examine. Twenty-five charges were preferred

against him, each more ridiculous than the other, so much that they were finally reduced to eight. These charges were so clumsily put together, with wrong dates, streets etc., that the judge asked him if he would like a re-trial and Bobby agreed. This was a tactical error on his apart. When the re-trial came up the police had time to alter and reduce the number of charges and correct the errors, and he was sentenced to five years in the Long Kesh concentration camp.

Long Kesh was once a military aerodrome and when Bobby Sands was committed there it still had its old Nissen huts, known to the prisoners as cages. This camp was probably one of the most heavily guarded in Europe. It was protected by an inner fence of barbed wire, an outer fence, two in-between fences and a fence around each cage. Coils upon coils of loose barbed wire several feet high were piled between each fence. Every seventy yards there was a camouflaged machine-gun post fifty feet high permanently manned. There was also a heavily armed roving foot-patrol with vicious dogs moving day and night around the camp. Each cage was comprised of three Nissen living huts, one Nissen hut used as a dining hall, church and a washroom. Constant searching and stripping had worn away the huts and on wet days the rain came pouring through. The food on the whole was bad and in short supply. In each hut there were approximately seventy prisoners sleeping in two tiers like the German concentration camps. Between each cage and the next there was no communication. However, one could shout across the wire.

Conditions in Long Kesh at the time would not be called those of a holiday camp. In 1974 Fathers Faul and Brady sent the following cablegram to the Red Cross at Geneva:

Visited Long Kesh today with others. Request immediate investigation by Red Cross into the use of CR and CS gas, war dogs and rubber bullets against defenceless prisoners, theft of prisoners' property and destruction of sacred vessels and vestments by British soldiers; scandalous lack of medical facilities, clothing, food and shelter. United Nations minimum standard rules grossly violated. Living in sub-human conditions. Britain telling lies.

This telegram from two responsible priests speaks for itself.

At this particular time the prisoners had what is known as 'special category status', that is, they were treated as political prisoners and had:

1. The right to wear their own clothes.
2. The right to abstain from prison work.
3. The right to associate freely within their own particular prison confine.
4. The right to educational and recreational facilities.
5. Full good-conduct remission on their sentences.

These concessions had been granted largely as a result of a hunger-strike by an IRA folk hero, Billy McKee. These rights were later removed in the British government's 'criminalisation' operation and Bobby Sands was to give his life to have them restored.

Bobby spent three and a half years in Long Kesh and during that time he matured and developed into a strong, disciplined and zealous Republican. He threw himself fully into every activity allowed the prisoners. On the one day a week when they were allowed to play football he showed himself to be one of the best players in the camp. He established what came to be known as the Long Kesh Gaeltacht, a small hut where only Irish was spoken and taught.

He read extensively and widely and performed the unusual feat of learning off by heart the entire novel *Trinity* by Leon Uris. Years later in the H-Blocks he was able to recite it in full, over a period of time, for his fellow-prisoners. As well, he began to learn his native language and eventually when he was released he had a competent knowledge of both spoken and written Irish. It seems as if the comradeship, the common purpose, the idealism he was to experience among his companions had the effect of steeling his soul and strengthening his determination to follow through to the end the goals he had set before him.

His fellow prisoners remember his flowing hair and winning smile, his boundless energy, his seemingly infinite capacity to master matters of the intellect, and his extraordinary grasp of the complicated principles of organisation.

His friend and fellow prisoner Danny Devanney remembers those days:

> His closest friends at this time were Gerard Rooney and
> 'Tomboy' Loudon, both now serving lengthy sentences in
> Portlaoise and H-Block respectively. They, like the major-
> ity of the prisoners were intensely interested in political
> developments. Bobby was always involved in discussions.
> He would read almost all the daily newspapers and would
> discuss each important point with whoever would listen.
> He involved himself in many projects, especially the con-
> cept of people's councils arguing the case for more republi-
> can involvement in the social problems of the people living
> in the ghettos across the occupied North.

After three and a half years Bobby was released, having
lost some remisson on account of being caught with an
asprin, and he returned to his home in the Twinbrook
estate a more mature and developed individual. As well as
making his services available again to the IRA he became
deeply and effectively involved in the social affairs of his
community. To help the wives and children of men in jail
he established a branch of the Green Cross. He joined the
Twinbrook Tenants' Association and became quite active
in their manifold operations to improve the amenities
there. Because of the inadequate bus service he succeeded
in getting the Belfast Black Taxis to run to Twinbrook. He
organised a weekly social club night for those interested in
native music, art and literature. He founded a newsletter
called *Liberty* to give voice to the ordinary people of the
area. In fact he became a kind of unofficial public representative of these ordinary people.

He spent this period of his life close to the helpless,
defenceless poor. He became their friend and served them
and they in turn constantly turned to him with their problems. He shared their lives and took their sorrows into his
heart. He was not only a political revolutionary but also a
revolutionary in the things that matter most to the poor —
patience, understanding, compassion and kindliness. He
struggled not only with the weapons of war but also with
the weapons of peace and mercy.

His sister Bernadette remembers those days:

During the months that he was out. . . his only time out
of jail in eight and a half years, he always seemed to be so
far advanced in his thinking. Everyone, even older people,
listened to him when he spoke. No matter with whom he
was he seemed to impress. . . No matter what it was, kids
in the estate committing acts of vandalism, or harassment
by the British, or people wanting ramps put up on the road
in case fast cars would knock the children down, the people
came to him and he tried to sort it out. He used to get on
great with the kids. . . he had great hopes of organising
youth clubs for them. During the six months he was out he
worked continuously in that estate amongst the people. . .
One morning he was arrested, him and Marcella, and they
were taken to Fort Monagh. He just stood there silently
and refused to give his name and address. My mother went
to the Fort looking for Marcella and Bobby, giving out and
saying this was a terrible thing. . . And the Brits said:
'You're not having him because he won't co-operate.' So
my mother and Marcella sat down and would not leave
without him. It had been pouring rain all that morning and
when the Brits released him it turned out that he had been
left for the whole four hours standing outside in the rain. . .
When he came home he took a chill and laid up on the
settee in front of the fire. But someone came to the door
looking for him, and he got up, put on his coat and away he
went. He just kept on going.

This period seems to have been the happiest of his life.
He had married his childhood sweetheart and they had had
their first baby, a boy Gerard. Sadly for all, this marriage
was to become another casualty in the Northern Ireland
war. He was fulfilled in the knowledge that he was helping
the people of the ghettos whom he saw as the step-children
of a horrible destiny. He tried to relieve the isolation and
agony of unemployed fathers, to comfort young children
living in terror of the British patrols, to greet with a smile
the mothers whose hair had lost its colour through constant
sorrow.

He went for long walks through the luxuriant wildness of
the rich countryside. The lovely resplendent summer was
unfolding the beauty of the surrounding northern hills, and
it seems as if all the loveliness inspired him to try his hand at

writing. At first he wrote only short poems and essays and then much longer works such as his prison poems so reminiscent of *The Ballad of Reading Jail*. What he has written surprised many of his readers with the depth of literary talent intermittently revealed. It was not, however, constant, and many distinguished critics bemoan the fact that he never really got a chance to develop these talents. While it is true that genius can write anywhere and does not require a state grant or university lectureship to do so, the simple fact is that he never had an opportunity to refine or perfect his work. Most of what he wrote was written in a stinking filthy cell the size of a small lavatory in which he was confined all day. He wrote with a biro refill tube in tiny letters on cigarette paper or toilet paper and succeeded bit by bit in smuggling it out. Yet despite all these limitations the great clarity of his mind and imagination, purified by his intense suffering, gave his words a meaning which even the humblest and poorest could identify with and understand. His death cut short not only a life of potential greatness but a literary output that might have brought lustre and glory to the world of Irish letters.

The joy of his short freedom, however, proved to be only an oasis in the desert, a sunbeam breaking through clouds of unknown terror. It came to a sudden and untimely end.

One day in autumn 1976 Bobby, together with five companions, was sitting in a car parked in a street known as Station View. The car was surrounded and searched by the RUC who stated they found a Colt revolver on the floor under the rear street. They arrested all the occupants. They tried to link Bobby with an explosion that had taken place at the Balmoral Furnishing Company in nearby Dunmurray but despite later scientific examination of ribs of his hair, pieces of his clothing, fingernails, etc. they were unable to find the slightest trace of evidence that would indicate that Bobby was in any way involved with explosives. Since I was informed that there was a security problem involved I was unable to ascertain whether or not the car was a getaway car, or back-up for those who actually carried out the explosion. However since Bobby was on active service neither of these possibilities can be ruled out.

Together with his companions he was brought to the notorious Castlereagh Interrogation Centre where there was a staff of special interrogators, many of whom were trained at the same barracks in England, where the secret police of the Shah of Iran were also trained in techniques of interrogation.

These trained interrogators were given the task of getting confessions of guilt out of prisoners and on the basis of these confessions it was an easy matter to obtain convictions in a Unionist court even though the prisoners denied the confessions. In a terrifying and disturbing book *The Castlereagh File* Fathers Denis Faul and Raymond Murray itemised hundreds of cases of the most excruciating torture carried out at Castlereagh. Worst of all perhaps was the fact that the men responsible for this torture knew that not only would their careers not suffer as a result but their prospects were likely to be enhanced.

The interrogators start by trying to break the prisoners' resistance by psychological disorientation. He is put into solitary confinement in a cell where highly sophisticated electronic equipment controls the level of noise, lighting and temperature. He is usually left without food for twenty-four hours. Then he is given a large meal and then a second large meal an hour later so as to distort his sense of timing and thereby upset his mental balance. Then the real works begin.

We are fortunate in having a detailed written account from Bobby of how over the next few months he was interrogated here. As well as that we have a magnificent long poem which he wrote dealing with this monstrous subject:

> I scratched my name and not for fame
> Upon the whitened wall;
> 'Bobby Sands was here,' I wrote with fear
> In awful shaky scrawl.
> I wrote it low where eyes don't go
> 'Twas but to testify,
> That I was sane and not to blame
> Should here I come to die.

He was put into a cell to await his turn, without his shoes:

> The floor was cold on stocking sole
> And boots forbidden things,
> For one might die if one might tie
> A noose with lacing strings.
> For tortured men seek death's quick end
> And branchmen know this too
> For stiffs won't talk so men must walk
> The floor without a shoe.

Part of the technique was to allow prisoners to hear others tortured:

> I heard the moans and dreadful groans
> They rose from some man's cell.
> And knew I then that this poor friend
> Had something big to tell.
> I'd heard him go some hours ago
> His step was smooth and light,
> But he'd come back like crippled wreck
> Or one who'd lost a fight.

Bobby had given his particulars and declined to give any further information unless in the presence of his solicitor. The police refused to accept this plea and decided to beat the information out of him. There were two two-hour interrogations during which he was repeatedly punched, kicked, beaten. There was an interval and the police started again:

> I was brought into a new room where there were two new detectives awaiting me. This was the third interrogation and was to prove worse than the other two. A detective stood behind me and one on the other side of the table. The detective to my left had been drinking and was very aggressive and violent. 'Before you leave here you will talk. . ,' he said. . . After each question the detective who had the drink would slap me heavily on the head, ear or face. . . This sort of thing went on for half-an-hour roughly with kicks and punches thrown in occasionally. I was spread-eagled against the wall with my finger-tips only high up against the wall and my feet spread apart and back as far as I could manage. The detective who was reeking with alcohol was punching me in the kidneys, sides, back, neck, in fact everywhere. The other detective was holding me by

the hair and firing questions into my face. . . I was told to
sit down, given a cigarette and soft soaped with promises,
deals, etc.

> They have their means and dirty schemes
> To loosen up your tongue,
> Some talk so sweet you'd think their feat
> Was one of pleasant fun.
> But soon you learn and soon you yearn
> For safety of the cell,
> For what was thought was penance taught
> Was but the gates of hell.

Suddenly the physical torture started again:

While the detective sat in front of me he was swinging his
foot and kicking me in the privates. I fell twice only to be
hauled to my feet in the same position.

> They chop your neck, then walk your back
> Spread-eagle you like pelt.
> For private parts their special arts
> Are sickeningly felt.
> They squeeze them tight with no respite
> 'Till a man cries for the womb
> That gave him birth to this cruel earth
> And torture of that room.

That same person — continues Bobby — was chopping
me on the back or the neck, the individual blows heavy and
continuous, about twenty or thirty times. I am not sure as
the other detective was punching me in the stomach and
yelling questions. . . I was given another cigarette and
asked if I was all right and told it was early days yet, so I
could make it shorter and easier for myself if I just put my
name to a piece of paper. . . I had been interrogated and
beaten for about seven hours. . . When I was told I was
going back to my cell I asked to see a doctor, but they just
laughed and said, 'You have some chance.' They also said,
'So has your fucking solicitor.'

> Now some will say in sweetest way
> They do not wish you harm,
> They try to coax, they try to hoax
> They murder you with charm.
> They give you smokes they crack you jokes

> Allaying all your fears,
> Then beg you sign that awful line
> To get you thirty years.

Bobby's narrative continues:

I was brought down the stairs into the interrogation building again. This interrogation lasted about two hours and was followed by another which lasted two hours. During both of these I was slapped, punched, threatened etc. . . After dinner at about 3.00 p.m. I was taken to the last room of the interrogation building. . . I was set upon by two detectives. I was punched very heavily across the head, ears, face and eyes. I was kicked on the legs. My head was smashed against a wooden wall. . . After this beating I was told to sit down. . . I was given a cigarette as if nothing had happened. . . I was then told that what I got was only a taste of what I would get unless I gave the right answers to their questions. . . I was hauled out of my seat and spread-eagled against the wall. Again I was beaten all over. . . I was then thrown down on the floor and told to do press ups. I refused. I was kicked several times so I started doing press ups. I was only able to do three or four. I just lay down. I was then hauled up beaten and beaten and beaten. I was disorientated. . . my two arms were twisted up my back for about ten minutes or maybe longer. I don't know what position they were in but they were being held together by just one person at one time while the other concentrated on hitting me. When my arms were released from this position I could just bring them down round to my front.

I was spread-eagled again but I fell right away every time because my arms were so painful. . . I was also made to stand with my eyes closed and punched in different places where I was not expecting to be hit. The interrogation ended at approximately 5.00 p.m. . . I was put back in the cell exhausted and in pain. The bright light still shone and the four walls depressed me. I got off the bed and walked up and down the cell, four paces each way. I was exhausted, pained, depressed and demoralised but I knew that if I didn't keep walking and keep my mind going that I would break down and sign my name to a lot of things I knew nothing about. I had been asked to put my signature on a blank sheet which I refused.

I was taken out that night again. I cannot remember

whether it was once or twice but I do remember an interrogation at 10.00 or 10.30 p.m. It lasted one and a half
hours roughly. I remember the time as one of the detectives
said he wanted to get home to see Match of the Day on TV.

This last chilling sentence reminds one of people like
Eichmann and Heydrich and the SS guards in the concentration camps who went home to listen to the radio or go to a
concert with their wives and families after a day of torturing
others, and who reported for work the next morning to do
the same thing. Incidentally, this account of Bobby's has
already been published in two newspapers and a book and
to my knowledge has never been refuted.

This whole question of torture of defenceless Irish prisoners of which Bobby Sands was only one out of thousands,
is the direct result of instructions from the British government which said in effect: *Get convictions no matter how.*

In 1978 the European Commission of Human Rights
found Britain guilty of 'torture' (but the Court later
changed this to 'inhuman and degrading treatment') of
Irish prisoners. Amnesty International found the same. A
number of English television programmes exposed this torture. Hundreds of signed and witnessed statements of torture have been published. Details of much of this is also
given in an excellent Penguin book *Beating the Terrorists*
by Peter Taylor which explains why the torture was not
stopped and exposes the subsequent political cover-up.
The Association of Police Surgeons of Northern Ireland
protested strongly against this torture and one of their leading members Dr Robert Irwin resigned. In 1977 a statement given by thirty Northern Ireland solicitors to Roy
Mason, the then secretary for the North, said: 'Ill-treatment of suspects by police officers with the object of
obtaining confessions is now common practice.'

An editorial of the *Irish Press* as early as 1972 strongly
condemned this torture:

The men who play out the role of torturers in the North
today cannot be excused. It is not enough that they are
obeying orders, acting within instructions. They are guilty

and should pay for their crimes. But what of the responsibility of those further up the line? The doctors and the generals, the official lawyers, and the civilian officials are also involved. And most of all the political leaders in whose interest and with whose authority these barbarities are perpetrated.

But they failed to break Bobby Sands. Despite all the torture he refused to sign anything. So in the spring of 1977 they hauled him before the court on a charge of having possession of a revolver even though they did not find it on him nor could they prove it was his.

No Irish political prisoner, such as Bobby Sands, appearing before one of these courts in Northern Ireland has much of a chance. There are several reasons for this:

1. *The Judges:* A majority of the judges were either members of the Orange Order or ex-members of the Unionist administration. Unfortunately most of these men brought their bigotry on to the bench with them.

2. *Evidence of the Police:* The evidence of the police or the army is usually accepted as being the correct evidence despite any contrary evidence put forward by independent witnesses. In practice this means that the word of a man in uniform has become in effect the law in Northern Ireland.

3. *Acceptance of dubious evidence:* If a statement of guilt signed by the prisoner is put in evidence by the police then that statement is usually accepted as correct. If a statement of non-guilt is put in evidence by the prisoner's solicitor then that statement is rejected. One procedure adopted by the police is to torture a man until he signs his name at the end of a blank sheet of paper — then they later type in whatever incriminating details they wish. This evidence is accepted by the court. If a prisoner produces medical evidence that he was tortured that evidence is usually rejected and the evidence of the police that there was no torture accepted. In one poem Bobby Sands wrote:

> The case was clear cut, cruel by fear
> And carved by hand of law,
> The hidden hand that choked a man
> His signature to draw.

> While torturous screams haunt poor men's dreams
> From deeds that no one saw.

The figures show that eighty per cent of convictions are obtained by statements of guilt signed by prisoners. This is by far the highest in the world and nobody believes that prisoners in Northern Ireland are queuing up to hand in signed statements of their guilt! To show the preposterous lengths to which this kind of thing can go I quote the case of a young nationalist girl. The evidence produced against the girl was her 'signed' statement admitting murder. *But this girl was illiterate.* This was proven in court yet the 'signed' statement was accepted as evidence and she was given a savage sentence of imprisonment. Later, however, she was released.

4. *Establishment of guilt:* Unlike all other courts in the free, civilised democracies, in Northern Ireland a Nationalist prisoner is generally presumed guilty. There is no onus on the police to prove it. However, the onus is on the prisoner to prove his innocence. In one of his poems Bobby Sands wrote:

> They do adhere to law, I mused,
> But that law is their own,
> It is a law unto itself
> Whose face is never shown.
> But I have seen it, yes I have
> And brunt of it I've known.

5. *Degrees of brutality:* Different judges allow different degrees of brutality as a means of obtaining signed statements. For example, one judge might allow punches, kicks, and hair-pulling while not allowing thumb screws and punching on the face. A typical example of how that works is as follows: A prisoner may show that in ten different interrogations he was tortured during eight of them. The judge may then say: 'I will not accept in evidence what you said during the eight interrogations. I will, however, accept as evidence what you said in the last two. I sentence you to fifteen years.' Bobby's poem is here revealing:

> 'My lord, I gave him pleasantries
> I gave him cups of tea,

I even begged him to confess
Upon my bended knee.
And after some more pleasantries
My lord, he did agree.'

'Sergeant, there seems to be some claim
That you forced him to confess,
And that you walked upon his spine
And beat him up no less?'
'No! No! My lord, that was his own
Self-inflicted mess!'

6. *Variation in sentence:* Another very unpleasant aspect of these courts is the difference in sentence given to Nationalist and Unionist prisoners. Some examples are: A Nationalist boy gets fifteen years for having possession of a bomb. A Unionist gets a suspended sentence for possession of arms. A Nationalist gets seventeen years for setting fire to an empty bus. A Unionist gets ten years for murder. A British soldier who murders and rapes a girl gets off free. There are hundreds of these examples. Indeed one can only describe as extraordinary the fact that the cases brought to court against members of the army and police resulted in an almost one hundred per cent acquittal. This must be a world record!

7. *Collective responsibility:* If there are six people in a house and one of them has a gun and hides it all six can get up to twenty years imprisonment for possession — even though five of these had no idea there was a gun in the house in the first place. This had been used extensively to send whole groups of Nationalists to prison for long periods, and it has been stated that in many cases the police planted the gun in the first place.

These courts, known as Diplock from the recommendations of the Diplock Commission are not regarded by the Nationalists as courts where justice is administered but simply as conveyor belts to send as many Nationalists as quickly as possible to jail.

In one of his poems Bobby Sands asks how men can be blamed for taking up arms against such injustice:

And men ask why men rise to fight,
To violence do resort,
And why the days are filled with death
And struggles' black report.
But see they not, these blinded fools,
Lord Diplock's dirty court.

Bobby Sands was brought before one of these courts:

That dock a lonely island there
And I a castaway
The sea around alive with sharks
And hatred's livid spray.
But no one seen the wrecks of you
Or knew not where they lay.

He was charged with the possession of a revolver even though the only evidence the police could produce was that the revolver was in the car in which he was a passenger. Despite the torture he had signed nothing. He and his five companions were given a savage sentence of *fourteen years* each in Long Kesh. He had expected nothing better. With great dignity and resignation he later penned the following lines:

The beady eyes they peered at me
The time had come to be,
To walk the lonely road
Like that of Calvary.
And take up the cross of Irishmen
Who've carried liberty.

As he was being led down to the cells beneath the building his heartbroken mother cried out from the body of the court: 'Good bye, Bobby.' He turned around and waved to her and at that moment a security man crashed the full force of his baton down on Bobby's head and flung him to the ground. This incensed the other prisoners so much that they attacked the scores of security men but in a few minutes, however, they were beaten and overpowered.

But that was not the end. The unfortunate prisoners were sentenced to twenty-one days 'on the boards'.

'On the boards' means being sent to a special punishment

cell in solitary confinement subject to possible daily beatings, and deprived of all human contact, as well as books, papers or cigarettes. Each cell is bare except for a wooden board bed, a concrete block to sit on and a concrete slab cemented into the wall as a table. Prisoners are not allowed to use the flush toilet outside the cell door but instead are given a chamber-pot which sometimes can be emptied daily sometimes not. In summer these cells are stifling hot, in winter freezing cold. There is a special punishment diet of two cuts of dry bread and a mug of black tea for breakfast, two small scoups of potatoes and a small ladle of watery soup for dinner, and tea is the same as for breakfast.

Twenty-one days of this was Bobby's novitiate to the new Long Kesh. His *Via Dolorosa* had begun.

5

The Prisoner

So long as Britain pursues the phantom of military victory over the IRA in Ulster the violence will continue and the search for peace will be in vain. Fifty thousand Americans died before we learned that tragic lesson in Vietnam and there can be no excuse for Britain to have to learn that lesson now in Ulster.

SENATOR EDWARD KENNEDY

No British government ought ever to forget that this perilous moment, like many before it, is the overworking of a history for which our country is primarily responsible. England seized Ireland for its own military benefit; it planted Protestant settlers there to make it strategically secure; it humiliated and penalised the native Irish and their Catholic religion. And then when it could no longer hold on to the whole island kept back part to be a home for the settlers' descendants. . . Our injustices created the situation; and by constantly repeating that we will maintain it so long as the majority wish it we actively inhibit Protestant and Catholic from working out a new future together. That is the root of violence and the reason the protestors think of themselves as political offenders.

REV. JOHN BAKER, Anglican Theologian, Chaplain to the Speaker of the British House of Commons, now Bishop.

The British Labour Party won't lift a finger to help us.

JAMES CONNOLLY

For the remaining few years of his life Bobby Sands was to be deprived of almost everything except pain and prolonged suffering. Yet these years were to bring forth in him hitherto dormant qualities of greatness, courage and determination. In a way he was an excellent example of Nietzsche's famous principle: 'He who has a *why* to live can bear with almost any *how.*' In the midst of the squalor of the prison his writings rose to commendable heights of beauty and sensitivity. From the dirt, filth and stench that was Long Kesh came some of his most inspiring poetry and prose:

> On others' wounds we do not sleep
> For all men's blood is red,
> Nor do we lick the poor man's sore
> Nor drink the tears he shed,
> For king and knave must have a grave
> And poorest are the dead.

And again:

> I fought a monster today and once more I defeated the monster's army. . . It was hard, harder today than ever before, and it gets worse every day. I know some day I will defeat this monster, but I weary at times. I think and feel it may kill me first. . . My body is broken and cold. I'm lonely and I need comfort. From somewhere afar I hear those familiar voices which keep me going: 'We are with you son. We are with you. Don't let them beat you.' . . . I need to hear those voices. They anger the monster. It retreats. . . Will I overcome it? I must. Yes, I must. . . Yes, tomorrow I'll rise in the H-Blocks of Long Kesh. Yes, tomorrow I'll fight the monster and his devils again. . .

During this period despite his sufferings he developed intellectually and psychologically to such a degree that his fellow prisoners began to detect in him the leader they awaited. He became their spokesman and negotiator and their confidence in his ability and trustworthiness grew with each day.

But things in Long Kesh had changed dramatically since he was last behind its wires. A new addition to the camp had been built. This addition was to achieve world notoriety under its new name: H-Block.

The British government had become very worried about the impact their Northern Ireland policy was having on world opinion. One aspect of this policy which was becoming particularly embarrassing for them was the abnormally high number of prisoners behind bars. This number had jumped from a few hundred in 1969 to close on three thousand in 1975 and it was generally accepted, particularly by the foreign media that, apart from the Communist states, no country in Europe had so many political prisoners as Britain. This was interpreted to mean that there was a serious political problem in Northern Ireland and that Britain's treatment of political minorities had little to commend it. Britain acted swiftly to defuse and negate this impression. She produced a new plan to hoodwink world opinion. That plan came to be known as *Criminalisation*.

In effect what this meant was that there would be no more 'political' offenders. All would now be classed as ordinary criminals, deprived of political status, and forced to accept the same conditions of imprisonment as those serving sentences for such civil crimes as rape, embezzlement, larceny, drunken driving, etc. In future prisoners convicted of political offences would be forced to wear prison uniform, forbidden to engage in their own educational activities, particularly the learning of Irish, and forbidden to associate freely. By adopting this criminalisation policy on 14 September 1976 the British government had great hopes of achieving two major and important triumphs. First they believed that now they would be able to say to the world at large: 'We have no political prisoners in our jails and we have no political problem in Northern Ireland.' Secondly they hoped that the prisoners, if they accepted this status could be seen to regard *themselves as criminals* and the British government could then say to the world: 'These people have accepted the imprisonment conditions of criminals, therefore they recognise that they are criminals.'

On both scores they failed. World opinion did not react as Britain hoped, and the prisoners refused to accept criminalisation in any form whatsoever. In one of his most memorable prose pieces Bobby Sands wrote:

> I am now in the H-Block where I refuse to change to suit people who oppress, torture and imprison me. . . They have suppressed my body and attacked my dignity. . . But I have the spirit of freedom that cannot be quenched by even

the most horrendous treatment. Of course, I can be murdered, but while I remain alive I remain what I am, a political prisoner. . .

When Bobby Sands was conveyed to the H-Block of Long Kesh he had a fairly good idea of what was in store for him. Already there were four hundred fellow prisoners in the camp who refused to accept the British criminalisation conditions. The conditions under which these prisoners were forced to live were so appalling as to be almost beyond description. Because they refused to wear convicts uniform their clothes were taken from them and they were left naked in their small cells all day long with only a wafer-thin mattress on a cold concrete floor. The only other piece of furniture in the cell was a chamber-pot. They were deprived all day of reading matter, radio or any association with their fellow prisoners. The general routine was that once or twice a day a disposal trolley came to the cells and the contents of the chamber-pots were emptied into this and disposed of in the camp waste lot. The prison authorities stopped sending along this trolley with the result that there was nowhere to dispose of the contents of the chamber-pot except on the floor, so that after a few weeks the excrement was all over the floor and when the floor was covered they had to smear it on the walls. They then began to throw it out of the cell windows but the warders wired these up. In such unhygienic conditions of stench they had to try to eat their meagre food and there is evidence to suggest that some warders in a fit of sadism urinated on the prisoners' dinners. On top of all this they were subjected to ill-treatment and harassment of various kinds. Two books giving very detailed accounts of life in this terrible camp are *H-Blocks* by Fathers Denis Faul and Raymond Murray, and *On the Blanket* by Tim Pat Coogan. These two books make horrendous reading.

Cardinal Ó Fiaich (then Archbishop) was one of the few allowed to visit this camp and in the course of a statement made afterwards he said:

Having spent the whole of Sunday in the prison I was shamed by the inhuman conditions prevailing in H-Blocks

3, 4 and 5 where over three hundred prisoners are incarcerated. One would hardly allow an animal to remain in such conditions, let alone a human being. The nearest approach to it I have seen was the spectacle of hundreds of homeless people living in sewer-pipes in the slums of Calcutta. The stench and filth in some of the cells, with the remains of rotten food and human excreta scattered around the walls was almost unbearable. In two of these I was unable to speak for fear of vomiting. The prisoners' cells were without beds, chairs or tables. They sleep on mattresses on the floor and in some cases I noticed that these were quite wet. They have no covering except a towel or blanket; no books, newspapers. . . They are locked in their cells for almost the whole of every day and some of them have been in this condition for more than a year and a half.

Of this truthful statement of fact the *London Times* said: 'Dr Ó Fiaich could hardly have composed a more comprehensive endorsement of the Provisional IRA position.'

But the viewpoint of a Protestant clergyman, the Reverend Robert Bradford, Unionist MP for South Belfast, was somewhat different. In a television interview he said he hoped there would be a long hot summer so that typhoid fever might sweep through Long Kesh and exterminate all the prisoners. When he was killed later, the Fine Gael Coalition in Dáil Éireann proposed a vote of sympathy and stood for one minutes silence as a mark of respect to Bradford's memory.

When he completed his time on the boards, Bobby immediately joined the Long Kesh protesting prisoners and found himself thrown naked into a small cell. He wrote:

> We do not wear the guilty stare
> Of those who bear a crime.
> Nor do we don that badge of wrong
> To tramp the penal line.
> So men endure a pit of sewer
> For freedom of the mind.

In one of his most poignant books, *One Day in My Life,* now published as a paperback, he gives us a vivid pen-picture of what an average day in the camp was like for a Nationalist prisoner. This is Sands writing at his very best.

104

It charts almost minute by minute his struggle to preserve his identity and to transcend the squalor which surrounded him. Written on toilet paper with a biro refill and smuggled out, it is a masterly account of human bravery and endurance and will certainly take its place side by side with *One Day in the Life of Ivan Denisovich* and our own John Mitchel's *Jail Journal*. Commenting on this extraordinary book, Noble Peace Prizewinner Seán Mac Bride SC has this to say:

> I wish it were possible that those in charge of formulating British policy in Ireland would read these pages. They might begin to understand the deep injuries which British policy has inflicted upon this nation and now seek to heal these wounds.

It was always a great day for Bobby when he got his letter from home every month, even though he was not allowed to reply to it. With one of these letters came three packets of tissues. This thrilled him because he could now indulge in his great luxury which was to spread the tissues over the excrement on the floor so that it felt soft like a carpet under his feet. One letter from his mother read:

My dear son,
    I hope your received my last letter all right. I've been very worried about you and your comrades. Is it cold there, son? I know that you have only three blankets and I read in the *Irish News* that many of you have severe 'flu. Keep yourself well wrapped as best you can, son. I'll say a wee prayer for you all, Your sister Marcella had a birthday party for Kevin some time ago. He was one year old. He is a lovely child. You haven't seen him yet, son, have you? Your father and brother were asking for you, and so was Bernadette and Mr and Mrs Rooney. I was down at the march on Sunday and there was ██████████████████
██████████████████████████████████████
██████████████████████████████████████
(Censored. The bastards! I cursed them.) Everything is going well, son. Maybe it won't be long now.
    The Brits raided the house twice last week and smashed

my new Celtic harp that the boys in the cages sent to me at Christmas. I don't think the Brits are very pleased at the minute, son with all the ████████████████████████████
██
██

their heads must be turned, son.

Your brother Seán was down in Killarney and there's slogans painted on all the roads and walls about████████████
██
██

████████ *(H-Blocks!! You bastards, I said to myself.)*

Well, son, I must finish off. It's started snowing. I hope you are all right. We are all behind you, son. I had the child up in the house on Sunday. He says he is going to be a Volunteer when he grows up and get you out of that terrible place. God help him. I'll be up with your father and Marcella on your next visit on the 12th. Well, son, God bless you all. I'll see you soon. We all miss you.

Your loving Mother

Bobby regularly commented harshly on the smug who kept their silence on the H-Blocks:

> Who among them could put a name on this type of humiliation and torture. . . How much must we suffer? . . . An unwashed body, naked and wrecked with muscular pain, squatting in a corner, in a den of disease, amid piles of putrifying rubbish, forced to defecate upon the ground, where the excreta would lie and the smell would mingle with the already sickening evil stench of urine. . .

It has to be said here that few, if any, of the Southern politicians who are now so vociferous in their condemnation of Bobby Sands opened their mouths to protest at this.

Bobby expressed these sentiments in strong, meaty verse:

> To dance and prance to love's romance
> Is elegant and neat.
> To wine and dine on red port wine
> Is such a tasty treat.
> To eat and sit where you've just shit
> Is not so bloody sweet!

There were times when he seemed to have a premonition

of his early death. He wrote:

> And poorest are the lonely dead
> Who stare at earthen sky,
> And rot alone in skin and bone
> Upon the spot they lie.
> But poorer still are stupid fools
> Who think they'll never die.

These penetrating words kept haunting my mind one beautiful spring day as I stood by Bobby's graveside in Milltown Cemetery, surrounded by myriads of other graves of young and old killed by the British army or by Unionist paramilitaries. There is something extraordinary about the atmosphere in Milltown Cemetery. Unlike many other graveyards it seems to radiate hope rather than gloom, as if it were giving some kind of expression to an unconquerable spirit. As I stood there in the awesome silence, I remembered another verse of Bobby's:

> And blessed is the man who stands
> Before his God in pain.
> And on his back a cross of woe
> His wounds a gaping shame.
> For this man is a son of God
> And hallowed be his name.

Hundreds of statements telling of the sufferings of Long Kesh have been published by prisoners both in the press and in book form, yet the Northern Ireland administration has taken no effective steps to refute them. They have contented themselves with issuing a formal denial, while at the same time giving the impression that Long Kesh is in reality a holiday camp. Surely if they feel they have been misrepresented they could permit an impartial inquiry conducted by some international body of standing. This would finally show where the truth lay.

Outside the camp the war went on with uncommon ferocity. The Nationalist paramilitaries, now well armed, hardened and disciplined, took a heavy toll on their opponents. Their targets were the British army, the RUC and UDR, the Unionist paramilitaries and all informers. One result of this which we are never told about in the media is that for the first time in history the Nationalist areas became reasonably safe from attacks by Unionist paramilitaries and the incidents of petty crime, vandalism, etc., dropped dramatically.

Another particular aspect of the war outside which deserves special mention is that of the shooting of prison warders. Out of the hundreds of these officers it could be said that the majority went about their unpleasant business in a reasonably normal way. However, it seems as if a substantial minority well deserved to be called torturers. In all the IRA shot eighteen of these men between 1976 and 1980. Some of these shootings caused a feeling of abhorrence among sections of the general public who knew nothing of the reasons why these men were shot. A particular example is that of Deputy Governor A. Miles. This gentleman had appeared on television and had given the impression of being a compassionate, humane, soft-hearted individual who was sympathetic towards the prisoners and had only their good at heart. He made an excellent impression on the viewers. The widespread disgust and even anger when he was shot came, therefore, as no surprise. But unfortunately the media did not give us the other side of the coin. According to the prisoners (and the target is always the best judge of the accuracy of the aim) Miles' television appearance was a mere propaganda exercise and in reality he was a prison officer who not alone assaulted prisoners himself but who watched unmoved as warders beat up individuals on his orders.

In some of his more frightening verse Bobby Sands describes the sentiments of the prisoners on the shooting of a warder:

> So bury him and let him lie
> And play your brass tattoo,
> But write above his marble stone
> 'Here lies a stinking Screw.'
> For if men knew what he had done
> They'd turn their backs and spew!

As 1980 dragged on Bobby Sands, and indeed many other prisoners who continued to endure the barbarous conditions began to feel that the pressures being brought to bear on the British government to restore political status were not strong enough. The senior prisoners in the camp now felt it would be asking too much of the rank-and-file to expect them to endure their sufferings *ad infinitum*. So it was in this mood that the idea of escalating the protest to the level of a hunger-strike was born.

This hunger-strike would probably have taken place much earlier than it did were it not for the fact that Cardinal Ó Fiaich and Bishop Daly of Derry were engaged in negotiations with the British government concerning conditions in Long Kesh. These negotiations went on for a period of over eight or nine months without any worthwhile progress being made. The only concession they were seemingly able to get was that the prisoners would be allowed to wear a civilian type of clothes *supplied by the prison authorities*. This, of course, was just another name for a prison uniform and was unacceptable to the prisoners. These negotiations seem to show how little influence a prince of the Church had with the British government and in the eyes of the Nationalist population reaffirmed their mistrust in non-violent methods as a solution to the problems.

The decision to go on hunger-strike was taken by the prisoners themselves inside Long Kesh camp. *They were not ordered to do so by the Republican movement outside.* In fact those on the outside pleaded with the prisoners *not* to go on hunger-strike. Gerry Adams, Vice-President of Provisional Sinn Féin, wrote to Brendan Hughes O/C of the prisoners pointing out the possible ineffectiveness of the hunger-strike which he thought could only end with the deaths of many prisoners. Hughes did not accept Adams' suggestions. Again Bobby Sands wrote to Adams: 'I know you are strategically opposed to a hunger-strike, but you are not morally opposed to it.' Gerry Adams replied: 'Bobby, we are tactically, strategically, physically and morally opposed to a hunger-strike.'

This exchange of correspondence is of major importance insofar as it proves conclusively that the British were lying when they put out the story that the prisoners did not want the hunger-strike but were being forced into it by what they called 'Provo Godfathers'. Unfortunately the falsehood was widely accepted, particularly in the South, and as I have already said was promulgated by many politicians who should have shown greater responsibility before they unwittingly became mouthpieces of British propaganda. The hunger-strike did in fact go ahead *without* the blessing or approval of the leadership outside.

On Friday 10 October 1980, the prisoners issued the following statement:

> For the past four years we have endured brutality in deplorable conditions — we have been stripped naked and robbed of our individuality, yet we refuse to be broken. . . we wish to make it clear that every channel has now been exhausted and, not wishing to break faith with those from whom we have inherited our principles, we now commit ourselves to hunger-strike.

From all those who volunteered to go on hunger-strike only seven were selected. Brendan Hughes the prisoners' O/C nominated himself as one of the seven and his position as O/C was taken by Bobby Sands. Bobby was to go on hunger-strike but did not do so on account of his appointment as O/C of the prisoners.

The hunger-strike started on Monday 27 October and much to the surprise of everyone there was a tremendous public response. Pressures began to mount in various countries throughout the world. At home in Ireland Mr Haughey promised relatives of the hunger-strikers that he would raise the matter at his forthcoming meeting with Mrs Thatcher, but there is no real evidence to show what really happened. According to Haughey's supporters he got Mrs Thatcher to give her word that she would grant enough concessions to end the strike. It is in fact doubtful if she paid any attention to him or if she simply dismissed him with her normal contempt for the Irish.

What is clear, however, is that by early December the British began to make positive moves to defuse the situation. Ever sensitive to world opinion they were beginning to feel somewhat uneasy at the number of large anti-British demonstrations taking place not only in Ireland, but also in Britain, the United States and the continent of Europe.

On 10 December an official of the British administration visited Long Kesh and read out to the seven strikers a four-page statement the gist of which had already been given by the Secretary of State, Mr Atkins, to the British House of Commons on 4 December. The official refused to accept or discuss proposals put to him by Brendan Hughes. The strikers then made it clear that they had no intention whatever of abandoning the hunger-strike.

Then on Thursday 18 December the British made a further move. They presented a thirty-page document which was not only an elaboration of the document of 4 December but which contained a number of explanations the implementation of which would enable the prisoners to realise their five demands. In what seemed to be a gesture of goodwill Bobby Sands was recognised by the British as the prisoners' O/C and given facilities to confer with the hunger-strikers and with other leaders in different parts of the prison.

The document was worded in such a way as to appear unyielding on principle but in actual practice to give the strikers virtually everything they asked for. On this basis the hunger-strikers issued the following statement:

> Having seen the statement to be announced by Humphrey Atkins in the British House of Commons tomorrow and having been supplied with a document which contains a new elaboration on our five demands which were first enumerated upon by Humphrey Atkins in the House of Commons on 4 December we decided to halt the hunger-strike.

And on behalf of the prisoners on the 'blanket' protest Bobby Sands issued the following statement:

> Dependent upon a responsible and sensible attitude from the British government in implementing their proposals, the blanket-men will make a positive response. We are satisfied that the implementation of these proposals meets the requirements of our five basic demands. Republican

prisoners will not be wearing any form of *prison* uniform and will not be participating in any form of penal work.

Thus the hunger-strike came to an end — only just in time. Had it lasted another two days Seán McKenna, one of the strikers would have died.

Although the prisoners were glad that the strike could be honourably called off they had no illusions whatever about the trustworthiness of the British. They realised that it would be the height of foolishness, particularly for a group of political prisoners in the grip of British forces, to regard the solemn written undertaking of that government with anything but vigilant caution. 'The history of Ireland is a history of broken treaties,' Mr de Valera once said and these sentiments could be fairly described as the sentiments of Bobby Sands and his fellow prisoners.

Unfortunately their mistrust proved to be justified. Once the strike had ended and the Christmas holidays were over the British reneged on their assurances and promises and started the process of criminalisation all over again. The callousness with which the British ruling classes regard the Irish was made quite clear by a later statement made by a British Minister in the United States. According to a news item in an Irish paper, he said that negotiations with the hunger-strikers was like the efforts of the authorities to keep plane hijackers occupied while the plans are developed to subdue them. A statement issued by the prisoners said:

> The British government are past masters of deceit and double-dealing. We were aware of this when we accepted with some qualification their document. We were dubious about the sincerity of their intentions but were convinced that even they would not be stupid enough to waste yet another opportunity to settle this issue.

It was expected that Charles Haughey, the Irish premier, would make a strong public protest, since the dishonouring of their promises by the British was also a breach of confidence with Haughey himself. But he remained silent. So too did the Northern politicians and the Catholic bishops, even though Bernadette McAliskey publicly asked them had they been 'conned' by the British or were they part of the 'con' themselves. Only Father Denis Faul, himself no admirer of the IRA, raised his voice. He warned the British that because of their 'crass stupidity and complete lack of humanity, generosity and plain common sense' they were losing an excellent opportunity to end the prison crisis.

As the unfortunate prisoners saw it they were alone and they could expect no help from the Southern government, the Northern bishops nor the Northern politicians, and they had been double-crossed by the British government. With that extraordinary courage, grit and determination for which they have now become famous, they threw down the gauntlet, faced up to the British and announced another hunger-strike. Their attitudes hardened like steel and this time it would be a strike to the death. They issued the following statement:

> We the Republican political prisoners in the H-Blocks of Long Kesh and Armagh prisons, having waited patiently for seven weeks for evidence that the British government was prepared to resolve the prison crisis and having given them every available opportunity to do so, declare our intention of hunger-striking once more. . .
>
> Our last hunger-strikers were severely blackmailed by a number of people and politicians who called upon them to end the fast and allow the resolution of the protest. The hunger-strike ended seven weeks ago and in the absence of any movement from the British we have not seen or heard from these people since.
>
> It needs to be asked openly of the Irish bishops, of Cardinal Ó Fiaich and of politicians like John Hume, what did your recommending ending of the last hunger-strike gain for us?
>
> Where is the peace in the prisons which like a promise was held before dying men's eyes? And who but the Brits are responsible for our state which is far worse today than it ever was?
>
> We the blanket-men, and we the women political prisoners in Armagh have had enough of British deceit and of broken promises. Hunger-strikes to the death if necessary will begin, commencing from 1 March 1981, the fifth anniversary of the withdrawal of political status in the

113

H-Blocks and in Armagh jail. We are demanding to be treated as political prisoners which everyone recognises we are.

We call upon all those who supported us during the last hunger-strike to again rally to our cause and we call upon those who sat on the fence to now see the intransigence of the British and the justice of our cause.

The last battle in the life of Bobby Sands had begun.

6

The End

If I should die tonight
My friends would look upon my quiet face
Before they laid it in its resting place
And deem that death had left it almost fair
And laying snow-white flowers against my hair
Would smooth it down with tearful tenderness
And fold my hands with lingering caress,
Poor hands so empty and so cold tonight.

If I should die tonight
My friends would call to mind with loving thought
Some kindly deed the icy hand had wrought
Some gentle words the frozen lips had said;
Errands on which the willing feet had sped
The memory of my selfishness and pride
My hasty words would all be put aside
And so I should be loved and mourned tonight.

If I should die tonight
Even hearts estranged would turn once more to me
Recalling other days remorsefully
The eyes that chilled me with averted glance
Would look upon me as of yore perchance
Would soften in the old familiar way
For who could war with dumb unconscious clay?
So I might rest, forgiven of all, tonight.

A. E. SMITH

For this new strike it was decided that all those participating would not commence at the same time and that it would be staggered with intervals of a week or so between the beginning of each individual fast. Bobby Sands, who was now O/C of all the prisoners, volunteered to start and on 1 March 1981 he refused to take food and so began the strike which was to end in his death sixty-six days later.

As I have already said there is correspondence and documentary evidence to show that the Republican leadership outside tried to stop the strike. They pointed out in a letter to Bobby that the British would let him die and that he should not go ahead and that the strike would fail with a consequent serious blow to prestige and morale. But Sands and the other prisoners were adamant. They would go on strike and die if necessary. There exists at the moment an extensive collection of correspondence between the prisoners and the outside movement concerning the hunger-strike. This correspondence is at present in private hands for safe-keeping and may one day be published. Here is one sad poignant letter, yet one of major political import-ance. It is from Bobby to his parents:

My dear father and mother,

By now you will be most disturbed at what is to take place. I do not want to make you anxious or cause you any more pain. What I told you on the visit I must make sure you understand.

It is no joy to any one of us here to have to embark upon another hunger-strike. All of us realise and understand too well the consequences involved and torment endured by all the families but we have no alternative — we have tried every conceivable means to avoid this action and to end this protest.

The Brits are cruel — they are devious and callous. They are trying to cloud the real situation by saying or implying that they are moving to solve the issue and that we are un-reasonable. But in fact they have only changed the colour and style of the prison uniform. The whole regime is as rotten as it ever was and we can live here in the H-Blocks for the duration of our sentences and face unparalleled in-humanities, torture and eventual insanity. Or we can fight back with all we have left — our lives. We would prefer to fight even if it means to the death.

Please try to remember I won't be on my own — there will be others — maybe not as many as the first time but that is our decision. It is time for us all to stand up and be brave. I know this may be particularly hard for you and my family but you will have to bear up to it and stand by me all the way. There is nothing I would be afraid of except I should die with my own family opposed to my actions.

Last Christmas was my ninth Christmas here in prison.

116

I've lost a lot because of it, including the wife I love and the son I love. Even so I would go back again tomorrow and fight because I'm not foolish, I'm not wild. I'm intelligent, responsible and hold ideals that generations have died for. I do not enjoy prison. I do not enjoy the thought of death. I have lost many close comrades — all my mates are in gaol or dead.

So please try and understand. I love the two of you very dearly. I am sorry if I caused you worry and anxiety for so long. I am sorry if I am doing so again, but I must.

The Brits will try and move on you and use you to try and break me. Therefore I need you to stand by me. Speak to no one except to say that you back our stand and that you know and have seen England's treatment of Irishmen. See the boys at the Centre — they will keep you right at all times. You should listen to them and help them as best you can.

Please understand that the hunger-strike is our decision — not the IRA or anyone else. Remember that regardless of what may occur the blame for this situation and for what may develop out of it lies roundly on the shoulders of the Brits.

I will write to Bernadette and Marcella and Seán. I'm feeling very bad mainly because I worry that you may break down and ask me to end the hunger-strike. But I know you can be strong — I will go on regardless and die with that in mind.

Remember I love you all very much,

Your loving son,
Bobby

Once again the British spread the rumour that it was the 'Provo Godfathers' outside who were exploiting 'poor Bobby Sands' and the other prisoners and who would cynically allow them to die for a propaganda advantage. This lie was promulgated further by Southern politicians. Mrs Rosaleen Sands reacted angrily in public to this falsehood. 'My son was not forced to take part in a hunger-strike,' she said. 'He is on it of his own free will.'

From the first day of his strike, Sunday 1 March 1981, Bobby began to keep a diary and kept it daily until the 17th when he had become very much weaker. His first entry:

I am standing on the threshold of another trembling world. May God have mercy on my soul. My heart is very sore because I know that I have broken my poor mother's heart and my home is struck with unbearable anxiety. But I have considered all the arguments and tried every means to avoid what has become the unavoidable.

Thinking of his mother he wrote a particularly beautiful poem:

> Oh! Cold March winds your cruel laments
>   Are hard on prisoners' hearts.
> For you bring my mother's pleading cries
>   From whom I have to part.
> I hear her weeping lonely sobs
>   Her sorrows sweep me by
> And in the dark of prison cell
>   A tear has warmed my eye.
>
> Oh! Cold March winds that pierce the dark
>   You cry in agèd tones
> For souls of folk you've brought to God
>   But still you hear the moans
> Oh! Weeping winds this lonely night
>   My mother's heart is sore
> Oh! Lord of all breathe freedom's breath
>   That she may weep no more.

From the start he seemed clear in his mind that he was going to die:

I am dying not just to attempt to end the barbarity of H-Block, or to gain the rightful recognition of a political prisoner, but primarily what is lost here is lost for the Republic. . .

Later he spoke to his mother about his motives. He said he was prepared to die for the rights of all prisoners but he had particular ones in mind, the young prisoners of seventeen or eighteen years old whom he knew committed no offence whatever but who had false confessions tortured and beaten out of them in various interrogation centres. He felt proud to die for them.

Each day he filled in a few pages of this diary. He was delighted to hear that his mother spoke at a parade in Belfast but saddened to hear that his sister Marcella cried. He had some bitter comments to make on Bishop Daly of Derry's remarks that the hunger-strike was not morally justified. He seemed to believe that both Dr Daly and Cardinal Ó Fiaich let the Nationalists down, not in any malicious way but simply through ineptitude.

On the third day the warder put a table in his cell and put some food on it. This was to be a feature of the entire strike — the tempting of him with succulent food. On the fourth day he began to feel weak but he managed to have a shower and haircut and felt much better.

Later he has a delightful piece about heaven. The hunger was obviously beginning to tell:

> I believe in God, and I'll be presumptuous and say he and I are getting on well this weather. I can ignore the presence of food staring me straight in the face all the time. But I have this desire for brown wholemeal bread, butter, Dutch cheese and honey. Ha! It is not damaging me because, I think, well human food can never keep a man alive for ever and I console myself with the fact that I'll get a great feed up above. . . but then I'm struck by this awful thought that they don't eat food up there. But if there's something better than brown wholemeal bread, cheese and honey, etc. then it can't be bad.

He describes the enormous amount of food being put into his cell but there is no way he will give in. He is deeply hurt and distressed when he hears that a young twenty-one-year-old girl was given a savage sentence of twenty years for shooting at an RUC man. He again reflects on his situation:

> I am, even after all the torture, amazed at British logic. Never in eight centuries have they succeeded in breaking the spirit of one man who refused to be broken. . . I may be a sinner, but I stand — and if it so be, will die — happy knowing that I do not have to answer for what these people have done to our ancient nation.

Once again he remembered his favourite bird. On Sunday the eighth he wrote:

119

> I am awaiting the lark for spring is all but upon us. Now lying on what indeed is my death bed I still listen even to the black crows.

Monday, 9 March was his twenty-seventh birthday. He had spent eight of those years in jail. He was thrilled to get a picture of our Lady from a priest in Kerry who had encouraged him in his right to take arms for his oppressed people. 'It is my birthday and the boys are having a bit of a sing-song for me, bless their hearts.' He was also happy at the large number of birthday greetings from his family and friends including a Mass bouquet with fifty Masses from Mrs Burns of Sevastopol Street which he received on Wednesday, 11 March.

By a strange coincidence as I was writing these lines (March 1982) my eye accidentally caught sight of a poignant little newspaper advertisement:

> SANDS, Bobby. Birthday memories of my dear brother, Bobby, whose twenty-eighth birthday would have occurred on 9 March. I love and miss you always. From his loving sister, Bernadette.

On Thursday 12 March he began to feel very much weaker. His weight had dropped to 58·75 kgs, but 'no matter how bad, how black, how painful, how heartbreaking, never give up. . .' Again he thought of the lark. On Friday 13 March he wrote in Irish:

> *Dá gcluinfinn an fhuiseog álainn, brisfeadh sí mo chroí.*
> (Should I hear the beautiful lark she would rent my heart).
> If I write more about the birds my tears will fall and my thoughts return to the days of my youth. . . they are in my heart.

On Sunday, 15 March he was overjoyed to hear that the second prisoner, Frank Hughes, had joined him on hunger-strike. On Monday, 16 March:

> I had a wonderful visit today with my mother, father and Marcella. Wonderful, considering the strain which indeed they are surely under.

But although they did not say so at the time Marcella and

his mother were shattered when they saw his appearance.
He was unable to stand without swaying.

The last entry in the diary is for 17 March, St Patrick's
Day. It is entirely in Irish. The last sentences translated
read:

> If they aren't able to destroy the desire for freedom they
> won't break you. They won't break me because the desire
> for freedom, and the freedom of the Irish people, is in my
> heart. The day will dawn when all the people of Ireland will
> have the desire for freedom to show.
>
> It is then we'll see the rising of the moon.

A strange atmosphere of poignancy and pathos pervades
this intimate diary. Bobby knew how powerless he was and
he guessed what the end would be. It is this strange premonition that gives it such a sublime tone. He writes with a
lovely movement and with the naturalness of a child. While
his body was losing its vitality his spirit was gaining in
strength and resolution. He touched on political things with
the sensitivity of a poet. His patriotism was merged with his
love for his suffering people. The tragic way of the cross he
staggered along during these last weeks of imprisonment
and death was that way which was ultimately to raise him
up and write his name 'among a cloud of stars'. In those last
entries he is bravely waiting for the world to come alive
with spring, to hear once more the lark singing its exquisite,
celestial melody, to see all nature blossom forth in the grip
of an enchantment that brought everything to life again.
But his hopes are tragically shadowed by the knowledge
that it is the last spring he will ever see, and that when the
lark sings again he will be no more. It was his farewell to the
world he saw so little of and loved so much. Like all men of
genius he had yearned for the impossible. He was to
succeed only in experiencing a tattered remnant of the
possible.

Towards the end of March a completely unexpected
event took place which was to have a far-reaching effect,
not only in Ireland, but in all countries of the world. Frank
Maguire, the Independent Member of Parliament for Fermanagh-South Tyrone died suddenly. This of course meant

an immediate by-election in a constituency where there was a small Nationalist majority. It was of vital importance here that only one candidate should stand in the Nationalist interest, otherwise the vote would be split and a Unionist victory assured. Frank Maguire's brother Noel, and Bernadette McAliskey initially indicated their wish to stand. But then came the announcement from Sinn Féin that they had decided to run the hunger-striker Bobby Sands, and when the announcement was made public both Bernadette and Noel stood down and threw their weight and influence behind Bobby Sands. The role of the SDLP in this election is not one covered in glory. They did not field a candidate for fear it would split the vote and have a bad political effect on their own organisation. Up to the last moment they believed Maguire would stand and were staggered when he withdrew. They did not want Sands to win but could not afford to come out in open opposition. So a lot of their supporters contented themselves with a whispering campaign exorting voters either to stay at home or spoil their votes. It was the old serpent of Irish disunity, so expertly exploited by the British, raising its head again.

Bobby Sands stood as an anti-H-Block candidate. In a personal message to the electorate Bobby said:

> There is but a single issue at stake, the right of human dignity for Irish men and women. . . Our protest and this hunger-strike is to secure from the British government an end to its policy of labelling us as criminals.

Opposing Sands was veteran Unionist Harry West, who had once before held the seat, and who had at his disposal a first-class electioneering organisation. Sands' supporters had no such effective machine but the extensive experience and wholehearted help of Bernadette McAliskey and other supporters with election experience was of incalculable value to them. The real campaign lasted little over a week. Everywhere the public were deeply impressed by the moving speeches of Marcella Sands and by the quiet dignity of Bobby's mother who sat silently on the platforms. Everywhere Sands' supporters were listened to with quiet, restrained respect, but it was generally forecast that he would only get a fraction of the Nationalist vote and that West would win the seat.

Sadly the British army, the RUC and the UDR carried out a steady campaign of harassing Sands' election workers and tearing down literally thousands of his election posters. The British administration refused press, radio or television access to Bobby Sands while not hindering West in any way. In Derry a young woman collecting census forms was shot dead and the blame was put on Sands' supporters. Sands' election workers on their way to a meeting in Carrickmore were stopped by the UDR, questioned and searched for an hour. Owen Carron, Sands' capable election agent, Francie Molloy, his campaign director, and Bernadette McAliskey were stopped, delayed and harassed by RUC and UDR patrols. Another of his election workers, Patsy Grant, was arrested and held in Gough Barracks, Armagh. Danny Morrison, Jim Gibney and others were also harassed and held by the police under the 'Road Traffic Act'! Everything possible was being done by the British army to smash Sands' chances and it is hard to believe that they did this without instructions from higher up.

Because of inexperience in electioneering and constant harassment by the army and police it was expected that Sands would poll between 12,000 and 15,000 votes and that there would be massive Nationalist abstentions because, according to the media, the majority of the Nationalists were not behind the Provisional IRA and would not support them. When the results were announced not only the British, but the entire world media, were stunned. The voting was as follows

Bobby Sands	30,492
Harry West	29,046
Spoiled Votes	3,280

The reaction everywhere could be described as electrifying. However unpalatable to many it was now clear that the Provisional IRA enjoyed the support of the Nationalist population in the North, and those Southern politicians who tried to say the opposite were simply lacking in the most elementary political judgment. The *Sunday Times* showed a more acute insight:

> The election result finally puts paid to the notion — wistfully fostered by Protestants in the province and by government spokesmen abroad — that the Provisional IRA enjoy no support.

Andy Tyrie, leader of the Unionist UDA, said:

> If a UDA man stood in the same election he would have been lucky to get five thousand votes. This IRA man got thirty thousand votes.

> Now we know — said Rev. Ian Paisley — where the Roman Catholics in Ulster and the so-called moderates stand. More than thirty thousand of them voted for the IRA Commandant in the Maze prison.

The pro-Unionist press nearly had massive apoplectic strokes. The *Sunday Express* screamed:

> . . . those 30,000 ordinary people turned their backs on Christian principles and gave their support to the forces of evil. By voting for the IRA thug Bobby Sands they have handed terrorism its biggest propaganda coup in a decade. . . They have shamed themselves, their country and their religion. And their attendance at Mass this morning is as corrupt as the kiss of Judas.

The *Belfast Telegraph:*

> What a tragic result. . . The Nationalist minded voters of Fermanagh and South Tyrone have a lot to answer for.

The *Belfast Newsletter* trumpeted the old sectarian tune:

> . . . Let those 30,000 voters be assured this morning that with them there cannot be, nor is there ever likely to be, unity of spirit. They have placed themselves beyond the boundaries of our civilisation. . .

Smarting from defeat the British government immediately sought legal means to unseat Sands who proclaimed:

> It is not republican hunger-striker Bobby Sands MP that is the problem, but it is Britain's foiled policy of attempting to brand Irish political prisoners as criminals which has your

124

government scurrying for legal procedures to unseat a dying man and which, if you allow it, will shame you in the eyes of the world.

Because there was too much opposition internationally Britain backed down and did not proceed with the move to expel Sands, but they did introduce a law to prevent prisoners standing as election candidates.

It was particularly distasteful to Margaret Thatcher especially as Bobby Sands had received ten thousand more votes that she had in her own constituency. Thatcher was a woman with an almost pathological contempt for the Irish, a bully, anxious to prove she was stronger than a man. Like a bull in a china shop — albeit with petticoats — she rushed into situations without considering the consequences. And then having found herself in a dilemma chose the 'strong male, masculine' way out. Unwittingly she gave the best description of herself when she said: 'It is a lesson every child learns at school — the bully sets upon the weak and not the strong.'

And so Bobby Sands, the hunger-striking prisoner in the hated H-Block was, to the intense humiliation of the British, the new MP for Fermanagh-South Tyrone. They were not likely to forget this humiliation. There were many people, including his family, who had hopes that as he was now a Member of Parliament in the Mother of Parliaments he would not be let die. But many realistic observers saw a different picture. It seemed to them that from the moment he was elected MP and had dealt such a mortal blow to British pride and prestige across the world his days were numbered. The British, they felt, do not forget or forgive so easily.

He was now front-page news all over the globe but at home the condition of his health was sinking rapidly. He had been removed to a high security cell in the prison hospital where he was allowed the privilege of having a radio. He was particularly thrilled when he listened to the news reports of the progress of the H-Block protests outside. One evening he heard an external broadcasting unit interviewing people in various parts of Ireland about the hunger-strike and was delighted to find that, with the exception of Galway, every area covered supported him. 'Sandy Row would have spoken better for me than Galway,' he said later to his mother. 'The West is still asleep.'

When his mother, father and sister Marcella visited him on 21 April they found his speech slurred, his hearing impaired and he was unable to focus his vision. As well he was suffering from severe headaches. The fillings had begun to fall out from his teeth. Each movement of his body caused severe pain. But he only smiled weakly and made no complaints to his family.

Down South a new development took place. Miss Sile de Valera, grand-daughter of President de Valera and European MP, issued a statement which was understood to endorse Bobby Sands' campaign. Later at the Fianna Fáil Ard Fheis she was given a tumultuous reception which was taken to indicate that the grass-roots of the party were behind Sands despite the milk-and-water attitude of the leadership.

Mr Owen Carron, who was Sands' election agent invited Miss de Valera, along with Mr Neil Blaney and Dr John O'Connell, three Euro. MPs to visit Long Kesh and see Sands for themselves. The visit took place on Monday 20 April after the necessary permission was given by the Northern Ireland office. It lasted an hour or so. Neither Sile de Valera nor Neil Blaney asked Bobby to give up his fast. Dr John O'Connell did.

> I did go out of my way to persuade him to give up the hunger-strike. He was very determined. I found that I could not persuade him. . .I saw in this man more determination than I have ever seen in any person before.

The three Euro. MPs sought an immediate meeting with Margaret Thatcher. Mrs Thatcher treated these with that special contempt the British ruling classes have for Irish politicians. 'It is not my habit or custom,' she said, 'to meet MPs of a foreign country about a citizen of the United Kingdom resident in the United Kingdom.' Apart from the insult Mrs Thatcher made it clear by that statement that she did not recognise any 'Irish dimension' as far as Northern Ireland was concerned. This statement of Mrs Thatcher was far more than just a contemptuous snub of the three MPs. It was a direct slap in the face to the entire Irish race in that it re-affirmed the claim of the British that a part of Ireland was theirs by right. The Irish government took this statement lying down and it became clearer to many that in all the Anglo-Irish talks it was Mrs Thatcher who was calling the tune and it was the Irish government who were doing the dance. She was still the overseer and they were the coolies, the white trash.

On 22 April, distraught at Bobby's deteriorating condition, the Sands family tried to get an interview with Mr Haughey in Dublin in the hope that he would make some last minute effort to save Bobby's life. *Haughey refused to see them.* Then quite unexpectedly the next day he telephoned and requested that they come to Dublin to see him. They travelled at once to Haughey's home where he told Marcella that the British wanted to get off the hook and that she should apply to the European Human Rights Commission to investigate. If this were done, he said, the Commission would go at once to Long Kesh and make an 'on-the-spot' judgment in favour of the prisoners. He then presented the necessary documents to Marcella who signed them in the belief that this action would save Bobby's life. Marcella says that Haughey threatened to wash his hands of the whole affair if she did not sign.

Sadly this hope seems to have been quite misleading. Three members of the Commission flew from Europe to London where they had a ninety-minute meeting with the British and then flew to Belfast. Bobby was now very weak. He had been retching almost continuously for seventy-two hours and he felt he should only see these gentlemen in the presence of the prisoners' O/C Brendan MacFarlane and two members of Sinn Féin, Gerry Adams and Danny Mórrison. Neither the British nor the Commission would agree to this. This attitude made Sands much more cautious and he refused to meet with them. He was very wary of this European Commission because in August 1978 the Long

Kesh prisoners lodged complaints with the Commission about the inhuman conditions. They did not raise the question of 'political status' yet strangely the Commission ruled against 'political status' which made Sands and his colleagues highly suspicious. Again he felt that the intervention of these men would be politically advantageous to Mr Haughey in so far as it would lead the public to believe he was seriously concerned and no doubt make his forthcoming election campaign easier. Shortly afterwards Bobby issued the following statement:

> The legal submission and request to the European Commission was made in good faith by my sister Marcella who was misled by Charles Haughey into believing that the Commission would deliver on the political prisoners' demands. Mr Haughey led my family to believe that the British government wanted a way out of the dilemma in which they now find themselves and that the Commission intervention was the vehicle for getting the British off the Armagh/H-Blocks hook. . . because Mr Haughey has the means to end the H-Block/Armagh crisis and has consistently refused to do so, I view his prompting of my family as cynical and cold-blooded manipulation of people clearly vulnerable to this type of pressure. The Commissioners' intervention has been diversionary and has served to aid the British attempts to confuse the issue.

As far as I am aware Mr Haughey has not refuted this statement although it has been said by some commentators that he genuinely misjudged the role of the European Commission.

The whole involvement of Mr Haughey in the Sands' affair needs a lot more clarification. He himself said that he had tried all means 'open' to him to solve the problem. I have not met any Northern Nationalists who would accept that statement. They would argue that there were many paths 'open' to him which he did not explore. He could have threatened Mrs Thatcher with the full breaking-off of diplomatic relations, or even more important still he could have threatened to end cross-border security co-operation which was then costing the Irish taxpayer over one hundred million pounds a year, and which was only helping the

British and the Unionists to copper-fasten Partition. Either of these or both together, it is argued, would have brought Mrs Thatcher to her senses. Haughey thought he had a 'special relationship' in regard to Anglo-Irish matters with Thatcher and this has been offered as an explanation of his obeisant attitude. But such does not appear to have been the case since she treated him with barely concealed contempt. Again on a radio programme he was asked if he agreed with Sile de Valera who had said that if there were deaths it was the responsibility of Mrs Thatcher, he replied, 'No. I would not say that at all.' Did this mean that he was on Mrs Thatcher's side? Sir Nicholas Henderson, the British envoy to the United States said on a TV programme: 'The Dublin government does not agree that the Maze prisoners should have political status.' This important statement by a responsible British official could only mean that Mr Haughey, as head of that government, must also have been in agreement with the British government. Indeed this point of view had an important bearing on the whole strike. No matter what foreign government tried to intervene on behalf of the strikers they were effectively silenced by Mrs Thatcher who was able to assure them that the Irish government was in full agreement with her in not granting the prisoners' demands. So far Mr Haughey has given no explanation of these inconsistencies. If he does not do so then he runs a grave risk that history will not be too complimentary to him. Many young idealistic Irishmen have seen in this failure to save Bobby Sands one more proof that Fianna Fáil had abandoned one of the main objects for which it was founded. This, of course, poses another *realpolitik* question: What options have been left open to such young men?

Another attempt to break the deadlock was made by Pope John Paul II. What the motives behind this attempt were is anybody's guess. In 1979 the Pope visited Ireland as a kind of curtain raiser to his visit to the United States and the United Nations. He is a man of great charisma but also a very shrewd politician. I did not find Northern Nationalists entirely enamoured of Pope John Paul II. They reminded me that in 1980 when the Queen of England visited him he said in the course of his address: 'The ideals of freedom and democracy anchored in your past remain challenges for every generation of upright citizens in your land.' Northerners wonder who in heavens name composed that speech for him, and where were the ideals of freedom and democracy shown? In Aden, Cyprus, Kenya, Palestine, Ireland? They interpreted his failure to visit Northern Ireland as an indication that politics and not pastoral care ruled the day.

His speeches disappointed Nationalist opinion by what was believed to be their carefully concealed slant and their failure to recognise that the war in the North only came after fifty years of failure by peaceful means. He pleaded, they say, with the men of violence to return to the ways of peace, but he did not use his powerful influence with the people who were responsible for the torture and who were really answerable for most of the violence. According to an article in the London *Times,* Archbishop Heim, the apostolic delegate, is known to have promoted the British government's attitude to Northern Ireland very forcefully in Rome and it is recognised that his efforts persuaded the Pope not to refer in Ireland to the controversy surrounding the H-Blocks. Archbishop Heim was subsequently appointed Vatican ambassador to Britain. Provisional Sinn Féin sent the Pope a courteously worded comment through the papal nuncio requesting direct contact with him. They got no reply or acknowledgement whatever to that request. One cannot therefore blame Bobby Sands if he treated any initiative from the Pope with the greatest of caution.

On Tuesday 28 April the Pope sent his personal secretary, Father John Magee, from Rome to Belfast with the object of inducing Bobby Sands to give up the hunger-strike. The powerful influence of the British foreign office with the Vatican for the past hundred years or more is well known and whether or not this visit was inspired by the British is a matter for conjecture. The Pope, it is said, felt quite confident that Sands, coming from a good Catholic family and being a practising Catholic himself would obey and give up the fast. It is somewhat strange that the Pope should choose this method of conveying his wishes to Bobby Sands. He could have sent his message with equal effect through Cardinal Ó Fiaich in Armagh or through the papal nuncio in Dublin. Instead he choose to send his special messenger from Rome amid a blaze of world publicity. Was there another reason why he intervened in a way that created maximum media coverage? Some *realpolitik* observers say there was.

For a long time both the Vatican and the British foreign office had been negotiating on the establishment of full diplomatic relations between both states. This would give the Vatican tremendous prestige in Britain and on the other hand would enable the British to pass their version of Northern Ireland affairs directly into the Pope's ear without having to go through the papal nuncio in Dublin. At the time of the hunger-strike negotiations were at a crucial stage and what better proof of his power and influence could the Pope give the British than the capitulation of Bobby Sands? This would have been a major coup for John Paul II — to have succeeded where everyone else failed — and would have enhanced the Papacy in the eyes of a somewhat suspicious British people, made a papal ambassador at the Court of St James more acceptable to them and eased the way for the papal visit to England in 1982. Of course, whether this surmise is correct or not is known only to a few but it poses the question: Was the suffering Bobby Sands being used as a pawn? If he was they had badly miscalculated. Sands with his extensive knowledge of history and his acute political perception — even though his body was shattered and devastated — suspected the papal initiative from the start. He saw Father Magee, listened courteously to him, accepted a gift of a papal crucifix but refused the papal request, and sent the priest on his way. Once again this young Irishman clashed with a powerful world force and emerged unscathed.

I remember discussing this whole papal initiative with an old woman in a Nationalist ghetto, who was well into her eighties. Her point of view might be termed the very essence of *realpolitik*. 'Supposing,' she said, 'that the Pope as the representative of Jesus Christ were as anxious for the life of Bobby Sands as Christ would be were he on earth, he could have told Father Magee not to arrive in Long Kesh in a Mercedes but to arrive there riding a donkey like his Master entering Jerusalem. Supposing he again told Father Magee to stand at the gates of Long Kesh, wrap himself in a dirty prison blanket and announce to the world that on the Pope's instructions he was going to remain there in the open, and not eat any food whatever until both sides came together and produced an acceptable solution. Can you imagine the world publicity this would generate? Can you imagine the number of TV cameras that would descend on Belfast? You may rest assured,' she added with a twinkle in her eye, 'that if this happened Bobby Sands' life would be saved in a matter of days.'

Perhaps the most insensitive, ignorant and almost obscene visit of all was that of a Mr Don Concannon, a former junior minister in the Labour Government and the man mainly responsible for the building of the Long Kesh prison. He came over from London to inform the dying Sands that the Labour Party in England supported Thatcher's stand to let him die. John Hume described Concannon's visit as 'a cheap and offensive publicity stunt' while the chairman of the Labour Party in Northern Ireland said that Concannon's visit was 'totally insensitive and like sending a British tank to a Northern Ireland funeral.'

But after all the dust of publicity had settled the sad fact was the British had decided to let Bobby Sands die. In those last days his physical appearance underwent a marked change. Owen Carron describes his last visit:

> Bobby was in tremendous pain and obviously close to death. I found him awfully changed from the week before. . . One eye was completely closed and he could not see from the other. He only recognised me by my voice. His mouth was twisted as if he'd had a stroke. His voice was distorted and he spoke very slowly and with great effort. His teeth and gums were protruding and he'd got a skeleton-like look. You could have spanned his whole chest with your hand.

When he said 'goodbye' to Owen he mentioned all his friends by name. He said everyone should keep their hearts up. He thought the Brits would need their pound of flesh.

'Tell everyone,' he said to Owen, 'I'll see them somewhere, sometime.'

Owen Carron kissed him goodbye on the cheek. A few tear-drops fell from the one eye that remained open.

By Thursday he had lost all feeling in his mouth and found it very hard to speak. By the Saturday his eyesight was gone and there was no feeling in one side of his body. His last words to Jim Gibney were: 'I'm extremely weak. I'm blind. I can't see. Tell the lads to keep their chins up. I'll see this thing through.' On the Sunday morning when his family came to visit him they thought he was dead. His mother knelt beside his bed and said an Act of Contrition into his ear. Bobby nodded and then rallied a little and prayed together with her, his hands folded around the crucifix.

During these last terrible days the Sands family were put through the full rigours of prison discipline. The parents were not allowed to stay alone with their dying son. All those long hours as they watched him die a prison warder stayed by them with a pencil and notebook and wrote down everything that was said. They were treated with coldness and indifference by the warders with one exception. This one man did everything he could to help them and to comfort Bobby.

On the Monday, the day before Bobby died, Mr Haughey's secretary telephoned Marcella and requested her to go to a hotel in Dundalk and make out a new complaint for the Commission on Human Rights. Marcella refused. She no longer trusted Haughey and at any rate it was now too late. Bobby had but hours to live.

Later Marcella wanted to make an urgent phone call out of the prison concerning her infant son who was being cared for by friends. She was refused the use of the phone but managed to contact a chaplain who drove her three miles to his house to make the call. When she returned later she was subjected to a humiliating search before she was readmitted to her dying brother.

About four o'clock on Monday evening there was a mysterious phone call for Mrs Sands but when she left the prison cell to answer it she was told by a senior official that she would not be allowed to take any calls. This official then said to her: 'Mrs Sands, I would like you to know that we have done everything for your son.' With quiet dignity Mrs Sands looked him in the eye and replied: 'This place has tortured my son for four and a half years and it has now murdered him.' As she walked away she could sense the official's rage and anger.

A final insensitivity awaited Bobby in his last hours. Outside the wall of his cell somebody, presumably security men, started pistol-firing practice. The constant noise of shots echoed and re-echoed through the dying man's cell, and at intervals when the shooting stopped a helicopter roared overhead. The family suspect that this could have been deliberate harassment. Only in the context of Northern Ireland politics can such appalling happenings be understood.

But nothing could sway Bobby Sands' conscience. He could not be bought or fooled by subtleties or browbeaten by harassment. The force that was driving him on was more powerful than all the armies of all the nations on earth. It was indestructible.

Owen Carron made one last desperate attempt to save Bobby's life. He sent the following telegram to Charlie Haughey:

On my final visit to Bobby Sands yesterday his dying request was that you publicly call upon Mrs Thatcher to give political prisoners their five demands. I formally lodged this request with Seán Aylward (an official in Mr Haughey's office) at 3 p.m. yesterday. Frank Dunlop, head of the Government Information Service, has informed me today that there will be no response. Why not?

Nothing happened and Owen Carron commented:

I relayed that message on Friday and Saturday but he has not bothered to reply. That shows us that Charlie Haughey is not really interested in the people of Northern Ireland.

He forfeits the right to be called leader of any section of the Irish people and he stands condemned at the bar of Irish history.

Before he lapsed into a coma Bobby received Holy Communion and the last Sacraments were administered to him. His family noticed an extraordinary aura of dignity and peace about him as he neared the end. No matter how much they wanted him to live, when they came into his presence they felt an uplifting fortitude and moral strength take hold of them and they were completely reconciled to his right to die for his fellow men. 'He was fully prepared for the end,' said his heart-broken mother, who had sat by his bedside hour after hour and finally minute after minute watching her son die. She promised him not to ask the prison doctors to revive him should he go into a coma.

'He told me not to,' said Mrs Sands. 'I love my son like any other mother, but I wouldn't, I can't. He asked me not to and I've promised him not to.'

Before he lapsed into a final coma he said feebly: 'I love you all', and to his mother: 'You are the best mother in the world. You stood by me.' These were his last words. In the early hours of the morning of 5 May the immortal soul of one of the noblest young Irishmen of the twentieth century came face-to-face with his Fellow Sufferer and Maker.

Bobby Sands was dead.

Epilogue

Those who do not remember the past are compelled to repeat it.

GEORGE SANTAYANA

In Ireland over the centuries, we have tried every possible formula: direct rule, indirect rule, colonisation, land reform, partition. Nothing has worked. The only solution we have not tried is absolute and unconditional withdrawal. . .

PAUL JOHNSON in the *New Statesman*

To have been destroyed by tyranny is the most beautiful epitaph of all

DIONYSIUS

Nine more young Irishmen were to die on hunger-strike, nine more coffins were to be filled before a settlement was found. Nine more heart-broken mothers were to stand over the graves of their sons and mourn them with sadness yet with dignity and honour. These young men were: Francis Hughes, Raymond McCreesh, Patsy O'Hara, Joe McDonnell, Martin Hurson, Kevin Lynch, Kieran Doherty, TD, Thomas McElwee and Michael Devine. Some months later when Margaret Thatcher's own son was missing on a desert jink the media presented her in tears while awaiting news of his whereabouts. As I looked at her distraught face on television I wondered had she spared a thought for the other ten sons in Northern Ireland for whom there was no return or for their mothers who had hoped and waited for so long.

Almost two years have now gone by since the deaths of the hunger-strikers and I think it would be a fitting end to this book to take a short look at what has happened since and what effect these deaths, particularly the death of Bobby Sands, have had on the affairs of this island as a whole.

Many of the prisoners' demands, which started the strike in the first place, have been granted, but couched in a phraseology sufficiently ambiguous to save Thatcher's face. Yet despite this there are still rumours that the day-to-day relationship between some warders and the prisoners in some prisons are such that tension between them might very easily erupt into another strike. I thought, therefore, that I should visit Long Kesh to try to evaluate the situation for myself. The Lord Earl of Gowrie is the British minister with responsibility for prisons in the Six Counties. Gowrie is a Southern Irishman who has placed what talents he may have at the disposal of the British and latterly has spoken in defence of the use of plastic bullets by the security forces. On 31 March 1982 I wrote to him indicating that I was writing a book and requesting permission to visit Long Kesh. Five weeks passed without either an acknowledgement or a reply so on 7 May I wrote again. Three weeks later I got an answer. This nobleman deprived me of the great joy of knowing that I was a worthy subject for his gracious condescension by not replying to me himself. One of his minions sent me a letter of refusal in which it was pointed out that Long Kesh was a maximum security prison and there must be a limit to the number of visitors. I could only conclude that I was not one to be allowed or trusted within the walls of this infamous establishment. This unhelpful attitude contrasted strangely with the attitude of the Southern Minister for Justice who facilitated my visit to Portlaoise prison in every way. However I managed to get what I wanted to enable me to assess conditions there without the permission of the Northern Ireland office or the favour of the most noble Lord Earl.

Broadly speaking life is much better for the prisoners since the strike ended. They do not have to wear prison uniforms, but can wear their own clothes instead. They have a good degree of free association and the prison work they are asked to do is mostly cleaning and maintaining the areas where they are living. They are also allowed weekly food parcels consisting of eatables and as many letters as are sent to them. But there is a severe restriction on literature, particularly on literature relating to Ireland and Irish problems. Some few warders are allegedly harassing the prisoners in a variety of petty ways, but this does not seem to be official policy, and the governors are held to approach their tasks in an enlightened way. Yet it is a sad state of affairs to think that if these conditions had been granted a year earlier ten prisoners and sixty-four civilians would not now be in their graves. But those responsible for this cataclysm still live. Their kind always survive. It is the less exalted who must die.

Yet however welcome this new state of affairs is it is a very uneasy peace which could blow up at short notice. The vast majority of prisoners believe they should not be where they are. They were convicted, they say, by biased courts on confessions obtained through torture and they know that in any other European country, outside of Britain and the Iron Curtain states, they would be free men. Such a mood does not make for docile prisoners, no matter what concessions they have, and it would be a fool who would forecast that the saga of Long Kesh is over. It may well be only a temporary intermission. The British, if they are still capable of learning from history, should not neglect to recall the lessons of the centuries.

The consequences of the death of Bobby Sands for the British government were more far-reaching and damaging than most political observers had anticipated. It was generally thought that the worldwide British propaganda machine could successfully stifle all but a trickle of the truth coming from Long Kesh and could treat his death as if it were the irresponsible act of a desperado. This crudely simplistic hope proved to be a cardinal miscalculation. Like bolts of blinding fork-lightning Sands' death struck the whole political world, not once but again and again in quick succession so that the powerful British propaganda machine crumbled before it in almost every country. Such things do not happen very often. Once or twice perhaps in the course of a century an overpowering truth-force propels itself like a raging torrent sweeping everthing before it in a way that most mortals find hard to comprehend. It happened once before in this century when Terence MacSwiney, Lord Mayor of Cork, died in a British prison after seventy-five days on hunger-strike. In those far-off days there were many people who did not even know where Ireland was, but who spoke the name of Terence MacSwiney. It had now happened again but on a much larger scale.

In the United States Prince Charles was publicly and privately insulted. Mayor Koch of New York told him bluntly to get the British out of Ireland once and for all. The visit of Princess Margaret had to be cancelled. The name and smiling face of Bobby Sands took over on the television screens of that country to such a degree that the prestigious *New York Times* now rates happenings in Northern Ireland in its top five international coverage ratings, where before it measured only an occasional comment. The mass-circulation *American T.V. Guide* wrote that the issues of Northern Ireland were initially unknown until the death of Bobby Sands. Since then Northern Ireland is top news. It was the same story in almost every country throughout the world.

This resounding blow to the pride of the British government panicked them into spending millions of pounds in an effort to stem the pro-Sands and anti-British tide. Scores of extra information officers were sent to the major capitals of the world to present the British point of view and to blacken the character and motives of Bobby Sands. It is sad for any Irishman to think that in this campaign they were assisted by the Irish embassies in the various countries. The embassies were of course only acting on the instructions of an Irish government. That they should line up with the British made many Irish living abroad feel embarrassed and ashamed. This, of course, poses the question why should it be so? This attitude would be totally consistent with the policies of a Fine Gael government, but why Fianna Fáil? The most likely answer again seems to be that Fianna Fáil feared the rise of a new national force in Ireland to fill the vacuum caused by their own abandonment of their earlier principles. In practising the art of political survival Fianna Fáil have never been known to look too closely at the actions or credentials of their bedfellows.

But the massive counter-propaganda effort failed. Bobby Sands had captured the imagination of the world and there was little that the once-powerful machine could do to tarnish his image. The failure seems to have stemmed from the fact that world opinion began to have gnawing doubts about the whole integrity of Britain. People remembered suddenly her condemnation for torture and inhuman degrading treatment by the Court of Human Rights. How come, they asked, that we are expected to condemn torture in Russia and El Salvador and to condone the same torture by Britain? Why should a rugby team be censured for playing in South Africa and not in Northern Ireland? All over the world there was widespread expression given to these doubts and it now seems as if it is going to take long years of expenditure of money and effort to even partially heal the damage done to the British image. The helpless lonely prisoner who died in Western Europe's last concentration camp had dealt a severe blow to the hitherto image of the Mother of Democracies.

In the aftermath of the hunger-strikers' deaths when the television crews and foreign journalists had gone the British army and the RUC intensified their campaign of harassment against the Nationalist population as if they were instructed to take some form of revenge for the demoralising propaganda set-back.

In their poignant sorrow the ordinary people of one area erected a rough memorial in the form of a plain cross to the memory of Bobby Sands. It took them a few days to do this but immediately it was in position the Brits came and smashed it to pieces with a bulldozer. All over the Nationalist areas of Belfast short epitaphs, artistically executed, began to appear on the gable ends of houses in modest expression of a people's sorrow. Then units of the British army came around and flung plastic bags of red paint against the walls of these houses to daub and obliterate the simple lines of sympathy.

Thousands of Nationalists' homes were raided by the

British army. Furniture was smashed, floor boards ripped up, religious and family pictures broken, pregnant women struck with butts of rifles, their menfolk beaten in front of terrified children, while one regiment in particular specialised in urinating in the hallways on the way out. These raids have been well authenticated and documented and they reached such a degree of ferocity that the Association for Legal Justice in Northern Ireland publicly accused the British army of wilfully destroying property and causing havoc in Nationalist homes. Despite the fact that virtually no arms are being found these raids have never stopped and they are a constant feature of daily life today in Nationalist areas of Northern Ireland. Here I would make the suggestion to anyone interested, and particularly to some of our voluble politicians, to go north and spend a few days in Belfast or Derry — not in the best hotels but in the ghettos. There you will see everything I have described actually happening. And when you return home the chances are that you will search in vain for any coverage of what you have seen in the media.

On the other hand, hardly any raids are carried out in the Unionist strongholds and one can travel these areas the entire day without seeing a British soldier. Yet the Unionists boast they have a hundred thousand guns in hiding there.

A recent development has been the allegation by responsible public figures of the existence within the Northern Ireland security forces, in addition to the SAS, of more than twenty 'murder squads' who shoot and kill without warning or trial suspected Nationalist paramilitaries. If this is true then all our hopes for peace or justice are in ruins. How now does one appeal to young IRA men to take the road of non-violence. How can one justify Southern Irish police co-operation with such hoodlum forces. Michael Collins' method of dealing with such squads is well known. Must be have another holocaust before common decency prevails?

To foreign observers it seems incredible that the British cannot see that this kind of conduct is only hardening the attitude of the Nationalist population and increasing daily the support they are giving to the paramilitaries. Again I think that if we relate this conduct to our own lives and ask ourselves what our personal attitude would be if a foreign army raided our home, smashed our possessions, used the most insulting language towards our dear ones and shot our children without warning or trial? Most sensible people would agree that harassment and oppression of this kind is counter-productive but unfortunately in this area the track record of the British, both here and around the world, has not been one of great enlightenment.

The death of Bobby Sands had a tremendous impact upon the IRA itself. It gave them a martyr with whom they could identify and from whom they could draw inspiration. He was one of their own and they saw him as a man who died a hero's death like Terence MacSwiney or Pádraig Pearse. It raised their morale and it strengthened their belief, which was also that of Michael Collins, that the power of the gun was the only language the British understood. They won the sympathy of thousands of young Catholic boys and girls who up until then were not committed to violence as an acceptable method. Applications for membership increased significantly but for security reasons they had to be selective. Nevertheless they were able to increase their membership of dependable personnel by at least one-third. Their striking units of five men now usually consisted of three veterans and two new members. Again Sands' death opened the doors of many more safe houses to them. As well it helped to fill their coffers with large sums of unsolicited subscriptions amounting, it is rumoured, to nearly a million pounds. In the year following his death the British slowly began to realise that the IRA had become one of the major and most effective military forces of the twentieth century. In an article on the hunger-strike in an American magazine the distinguished writer Anthony Sommers said:

> In the Provisional IRA the British have been fighting the most persistent, ruthless guerrillas in history. Northern Ireland may well be rapidly becoming Britain's Vietnam.

One of the IRA explained their attitude to me:

There is no way the British are going to break us. In order to obtain any social justice we simply have to destroy the Northern state and unite the country by any means open to us. We have as good a right, if not better, to do this as Pearse, De Valera, Collins and the other leaders had in the past. There is no difference between their methods and ours. Orangeism will never be halted by negotiation. It will only be halted by force, and even if the struggle has to go on for the next twenty, thirty, fifty years, we are ready for it. Remember that the IRA of today were only children in 1969 when the troubles started. We are now an ongoing and continuing force — and this is something that never before happened in the history of Ireland.

It is a basic law of life, particularly of political life, that every action produces a reaction. In this case the reaction of the renewed vigour of the paramilitaries was the intensification of the joint campaign against them by the security forces of both North and South. The highly controversial cross-border co-operation increased and the Irish government activated the Criminal Jurisdiction Act and tried and sentenced Irishmen for alleged offences committed in Britain and in the North, much the same as if the French or West German governments tried and sentenced their citizens for offences committed in Russia. The appalling injustice of this legislation is a major matter of concern for quite a large body of responsible opinion for it is now clear that the Queen's writ runs throughout the Irish Republic. Will the paramilitaries now retaliate by shooting judges, witnesses and civil servants? If so we might well have a civil war on our hands. Could it be that the British have manoeuvred Lynch, Fitzgerald and Haughey into this position knowing full well that a civil war would be the result? It would not be the first time the British set us at each other's throats. Every Irish politician to whom the destiny of the Irish people has been entrusted might usefully meditate carefully on the words of the late Lord Birkenhead: 'War by the Irish on the Irish is the kind of political development which I observe with great pleasure.'

In Southern Ireland the impact of Bobby Sands' death resulted in a re-awakening of the strong nationalistic

143

republican emotions of a significant section of the population. The anger of this section at what was seen as Charlie
Haughey's fawning attitude towards the British lost the
Fianna Fáil party the general election and put them once
more on the opposition benches. During the election campaign he supported Thatcher's brutal approach to the
hunger-strikers by refusing to criticise her on any score.
The hard fact seems to be that she had 'conned' him up to
the eyes by fooling him into believing that they had a
'special relationship' when in reality all she wanted was
more concessions from him on border security. These concessions he gave, and they are now costing the Irish taxpayer two hundred million pounds per annum. In return
she gave him nothing except a taste of her arrogance. In her
eyes he was simply a policeman there to do her bidding.

In his book *The Rise and Decline of Fianna Fáil* Kevin
Boland says:

> . . . we still deploy with ever-increasing efficiency the full
> resources of our Security Forces along the Border. . .
> where they act on our behalf in concert with Her Majesty's
> army, Her Majesty's Ulster Defence Regiment, Her
> Majesty's Royal Ulster Constabulary to defend the integ-
> rity of Her Majesty's Realm part of which is defined in the
> Irish Constitution as part of our national territory which is
> still pending re-integration.

Mr Haughey has now gone republican again but history
is unlikely to judge him by his 'green' speeches but rather
by his actions — especially in the matter of Border co-operation — whether he is prepared to stand up to the British as
would become a man who has stepped into the shoes of the
men who founded the state — that is if he is still in politics!

Sands' death seemed to have no impact on the Fine Gael
party. Over and over again since the foundation of the
state, they have failed to learn even the simplest political
lessons. They continue along in their traditional role of
believing that Ireland's best interest lies within the British
sphere of influence. Their present leader Garret Fitzgerald
had been described as a man of obvious sincerity and
honesty, who unfortunately manifests an incredible politi-

cal stupidity in matters concerning the North — a man who talks too much and thinks too little. He wants to remove the sections of our Constitution which lay claim to our entire national territory as a sop to the Unionists, ignoring the fact that even if the Unionists were allowed to rewrite our Constitution they would not be interested since they are an inflexible group who care only for their own power and privilege and material possessions. It is as if the leaders of the Democratic or Republican parties in the United States started a crusade to change the constitution in order to woo the Mafia or the Klu-Klux-Klan. A *Daily Telegraph* columnist commenting on this crusade of Fitzgerald said that all the removal of these articles would do is 'to hasten the process by which the Irish Republic is becoming more and more assimilated to Great Britain.' He wants too, a federal police force which would include members of the RUC which any child could tell him must be the most bigoted police force in Western Europe. Again he wants an all-Ireland court with judges drawn from North and South. Looking at the present and past record of the majority of the judiciary of Northern Ireland there are very few who would feel confident in the impartiality of such a court. The British want a government in Dublin which will co-operate fully with them in all major political matters. They believe that a Fine Gael government would come nearest to that hope, and if one is to judge by Fitzgerald's utterances their assessment of the situation does not seem to be far wrong. It is quite noteworthy that the British press which vilified every Irish leader — O'Connell, Parnell, Pearse, Collins, De Valera — is loud and fulsome in its praise of Fitzgerald. It is almost unbelievable that neither he nor his close associates seem to realise that Irishmen have nothing to gain by going on their knees and begging the English ruling classes to notice them as a mark of their favour. It is, however, only fair to say that quite a substantial section of the grass-roots of the Fine Gael party do not subscribe to any subservient ideas, and are far closer to the traditions of Michael Collins than are their leaders.

I have tried to show throughout this book that Bobby

Sands is a symbol, a microcosm of the whole tragedy of Northern Ireland today. Far from being the criminal Mrs Thatcher called him, he, and so many like him, are all the victims of the first tier of violence that I have already mentioned — the Violence of Injustice — and those responsible are primarily the British, and then the Unionists and the Dublin governments. Bobby Sands is in his grave. So are thousands of others including many young British soldiers sent over here who did not have a clue why they were sent or what they were asked to fight and die for. But they died — and also like Bobby Sands — they left broken-hearted mothers and families behind them.

But those who caused all this will survive while the thousands die. Every time I think of these people I find it hard to restrain my anger and fury. At times I yearn for the burning words of a Zola or Swift to condemn and denounce them from the hilltops, because I cannot help thinking, and I must say it, that they are the real villians. But I know my protest will be of no avail. As the years pass some of them will be graciously received in Buckingham Palace and have titles conferred upon them. Others here at home will be honoured by university degrees *honoris causa*. But all will live out their lives on most liberal pensions, laden with favours and tokens of official esteem and it is unlikely that they will ever spare a thought for the thousands of victims who were sent to early graves either directly or indirectly through their political errors. That thought alone is sufficient to make even the most hardened agnostic believe in a Day of General Judgement.

There is an old proverb which says that when nature makes a man of real greatness she destroys the mould. The Bobby Sands' mould must now be surely broken and it is unlikely another one will be cast for a long time. There are those who are born great and others who have greatness unexpectedly thrust upon them. In his life Bobby Sands combined both most fully and most nobly. Whether or not one believes in his political philosophy or in the means he chose to achieve it, one cannot but admire him. Together with his companions he resisted injustice despite the most

146

powerful pressures that this world could apply — the Churches, the British empire, the European parliament, the Irish politicians—who sided against him in pursuit of their own political needs. Yet in the end it was he who was the victor and they the vanquished. The world now bows its head before the man it could not break. Few throughout the painful and bloody history of our country so perfectly fitted the famous words of another hunger-striker, Lord Mayor MacSwiney, who said: 'Not all the armies of all the empires of the earth can crush the spirit of one true man, and that man will prevail.'

But when all is said and done and the dust of those traumatic days settled, the hard, bitter reality is that Bobby Sands is dead. There is a terrible finality about death which only those who loved him most dearly and are left behind can fully understand. While the world may applaud and admire his dignified and matchless courage, we should not forget that in a fond home in Twinbrook estate in Belfast, his family, whom he loved so much, mourn him not only as a world hero, but as a lovable and affectionate part of themselves who is lost to them forever. The death of a loved one is the cruelest and most savage blow.that life can inflict and there are few words that human beings compose which can in any way reach the sorrowing aching hearts of those left behind. The only thing an outsider can do is allow and help them express their grief in their own way in the inner reaches of their being. But that terrible pain of loss will never really end.

The Sands family experienced the anguish and heartache of those harrowing nerve-racking months as Bobby lay dying, relieved at times by the hope that reason, understanding and common decency might prevail, only to have these hopes dashed again and again by a mulish pigheadedness with few equals in the history of free countries. They watched agonisingly by his bedside as his life ebbed nearer to its close, bringing what little comfort they could to his wasted, torn body.

And surely the deepest pain of all must have been felt by his dignified mother who brought him as her first-born into

147

this world, tended him as a child, encourged him as a youth, supported him as a man and who in the end watched him die a terrible death. Perhaps then in her honour, it would be a fitting close to this tragic book to quote the words put into the mouth of another mother by an earlier Irish hero which he wrote in his prison cell just before he and his brother faced a British firing squad:

> I do not grudge them, Lord, I do not grudge
> My two strong sons that I have seen go out
> To break their strength and die, they and a few,
> In bloody protest for a glorious thing.
> They shall be spoken of among their people,
> The generations shall remember them,
> And call them blessed;
> But I will speak their names to my own heart
> In the long nights;
> The little names that were familiar once
> Round my dead hearth.
> Lord, thou art hard on mothers;
> We suffer in their coming and their going;
> And tho' I grudge them not, I weary, weary
> Of the long sorrow — And yet I have my joy;
> My sons were faithful and they fought.

A Reading List

Between books, pamphlets, reports, etc. I consulted well over one hundred publications while I was writing this book. Here, however, I am only going to suggest a small number of books which will help the interested reader to get a clear perspective of the whole Northern Ireland question. It may be said that the books I mention here tend to give one side of the story. This is correct for the very good reason that ninety-five per cent of the serious books published on Northern Ireland are highly critical of the British and the Unionists. It seems as if they find it difficult to get any writers of standing to espouse their cause. On the other hand seventy-five per cent of media news is favourable to the British and the Unionists. How come the difference? It seems as if the British propaganda machine is geared to influence hard-pressed working journalists on the assumption that they are easier to sway and that in the end far more people read newspapers than books. The results would seem to vindicate this policy. Writers of books tend to proceed slowly and carefully and to check and double check every point of importance. They are therefore much less susceptible to the influence of a propaganda machine. Of course in Southern Ireland the public can only get the British and Unionist point of view on radio and television. Section 31 of the Broadcasting Act prevents them getting any other despite the strong protests of radio and television journalists.

The reading list given here will present a point of view not generally presented by the media. I believe it to be essential that anyone interested in Northern Ireland affairs should read these books. By so doing they will be helped very much in making up their own minds as to where the truth really is. It is only by examining both sides that one can be said to have a truly informed opinion — an opinion worth listening to.

Michael Farrell's book *Northern Ireland: The Orange State* (Pluto) gives the best political history of the founding of the state to the mid-seventies.

Ten Years in Northern Ireland by Kevin Boyle, T. Hadden and P. Hilliard (Cobden Trust) gives an account of the legal control of political violence.

Another Cobden Trust publication *Justice in Northern Ireland* studies the whole question of the actual administration of justice in the North.

Very good Penguin Books are *Political Murder in Northern Ireland* by Martin Dillon and Denis Lehane, *Beating the Terrorists* by Peter Taylor, *Ulster* by the *Sunday Times* 'Insight' team and *The Guinea Pigs* by John McGuffin. McGuffin's other book *Internment* (Anvil) gives a good account of how this type of detainment works and the brutalities associated with it.

Eamon McCann's book *War and an Irish Town* (Pluto) is a classic account of what it is like to grow up as a Nationalist under British rule in Northern Ireland.

James Kelly's *Genesis of Revolution* describes the collaboration of the British and Irish governments in maintaining the statelet, and Kevin Boland's *The Rise and Decline of Fianna Fáil* (Mercier) is an excellent account of the betrayal of the Nationalist population of the North by Fianna Fáil.

On the Blanket (Ward River) is Tim Pat Coogan's book on Long Kesh and greatly helped to bring conditions there to the notice of the world.

Too Long a Sacrifice (Dodd Mead) by Jack Holland gives a unique political analysis of the entire struggle.

The Longest War (Brandon) by American author Kevin Kelley is probably one of the best all-round accounts of happenings in the North.

A recent book *Contact* by a British army captain, A. F. N. Clarke (Secker & Warburg) gives a very revealing account of the workings of the British army in Northern Ireland.

The various books of Fathers Faul and Murray are absolutely essential reading. They are *British Army and*

Special Branch Brutalities, The RUC: The Black and Blue Book, SAS Terrorism, Long Kesh, Rubber and Plastic Bullets and *The H-Blocks*. These books are available from St Patrick's Academy, Dungannon, Co. Tyrone.

Other important books issued by the Information on Ireland Office, 1 North End Road, London W14 are *The British Media and Ireland, British Soldiers Speak out on Ireland, Voices for Withdrawal* and *Silent Too Long*.

One Day in My Life by Bobby Sands is published by The Mercier Press who will also issue *The Literary Writings of Bobby Sands* in 1983.

In the matter of periodicals *An Phoblacht* is the organ of Sinn Féin and gives a great deal of information which does not appear in the daily papers. Again it is important reading for any student of Northern Ireland affairs anxious to get the Republican point of view. Three other journals deserve special mention — the English *New Statesman* and the Irish *Magill Magazine*, and the new magazine *Phoenix*. These seem to have successfully resisted being influenced by the British propaganda machine. Their articles on Northern Ireland are generally very good.

I have tried to keep the list to a minimum but a study of what I have suggested here may help the reader to clarify many issues and to reach an all-round view of Northern Ireland, not usually given by the media in general.

A Short Glossary

Anglo-Irish War — the war between the IRA and the British army commencing in 1916 and ending with the Treaty in 1921.

Civil War — the war between the IRA and the Pro-Treaty Forces 1922-1923.

Dáil Éireann — the Irish house of parliament.

Fianna Fáil — a political party founded in 1926 by Eamon de Valera and comprising mainly of members who opposed the Treaty and who classified themselves as Republicans. The majority of the IRA who fought against the Treaty forces joined it.

Fine Gael — a political party comprised in the main of those who supported the Treaty. They were originally known as Cumann na nGaedheal.

Green Cross — an organistion which helps relatives of political prisoners.

House of Commons — the British house of parliament in London.

SDLP — the Social Democrat and Labour Party – a political party committed to non-violence which would broadly reflect certain sections of Nationalist opinion.

Taoiseach — the Irish prime minister.

TD — Teachta Dála – a member of the Irish parliament.

UDA, UVF, UFF — Ulster Defence Association, Ulster Volunteer Force, Ulster Freedom Fighters. These are different Unionist groups and should not be confused with the UDR.

UDR — Ulster Defence Regiment. A kind of home-guard regiment of part-time soldiers attached to the British army in the North. It is composed, though not entirely, of large numbers of the disbanded B Specials.

www.ingramcontent.com/pod-product-compliance
Lightning Source LLC
Chambersburg PA
CBHW021404090426
42742CB00009B/1002